HAPPY GOLF STARTS HERE

Creating a Foundation of Confidence, Consistency, and Fun.

Bryan Skavnak

Foreword by Olivia Lansing Herrick

Contents

Foreword

by Olivia Lansing Herrick

I started playing golf when I was 8. I wasn't a huge fan — too hot, too complicated, too boring, too hard. I stuck around primarily for the snacks, but also because I loved hanging out with my dad, and he loved bribing me to come to the course with him. Typically with Snickers bars. It was a pretty perfect arrangement.

Snapshot of the next 6 years of my life: I couldn't see, so I got glasses. I started buttoning my uniform shirt up to the top button. I wrote killer book reports.

So, I was a glasses-wearing, top button buttoning middle school girl who really liked golf. I'll let you imagine the magnitude of my social network during those years. Luckily, I went to a school that celebrated and encouraged being exactly who you are, and I made it through middle school unscathed. By the time I hit high school, I was the only girl who played golf at my school, so I played alone. Then I played on the boys team, which, as a 15 year old, was exactly as uncomfortable as you would imagine it would be.

I also played soccer and basketball. My parents believed in the opposite of specializing. I had to play a sport a season — no exceptions. They wanted me to have a thirst for golf that I wouldn't have had practicing year-round. I hung up my clubs from September until March. I played in our homecoming soccer games, and our spirit night basketball games. It made me a better athlete, better person and better teammate. They wanted me to fall in love with golf at my own pace. And a few hundred Snickers bars later, I did.

My senior year of high school, I was recruited to play for Drake University on their inaugural women's golf team. So at 18, me and my four other teammates began to write the (often comedic) story of women's golf at Drake. It was truly the experience of a lifetime, and to this day my teammates are my dearest friends.

The spring of my junior year at Drake, we hosted the Missouri Valley Conference Championship in a little town about 45 minutes away from Des Moines called Panora. Since the odds are you haven't been there, I'll paint you a very quick mental picture: little resort on a lake + 30 mph winds + cornfields.

Lots of cornfields.

I had won the conference tournament the year before and was coming off of a good junior season — a few wins and a handful of top five finishes. My first round was a forgettable 75, and my second was a stressful 69. I was leading by one going into the final round and a handful of strokes at the turn.

I remember walking toward the 10th tee box and feeling like I was in a great position. I wholeheartedly believed that if I continued to play smart, boring golf, I would drive home at the end of the day as a two-time champion.

And then I promptly made a 10 on #10.

The horrible details of how exactly it happened are not especially relevant in this particular moment, so I'll bypass the bloodshed and move on. But let's just say that I was 130 yards out hitting my third shot into a par five ... and I made a 10.

I literally made a 10. As in 1, 2, 3, 4, 5, 6, 7, 8, 9, 10.

And I lost by 1.

I don't have a lot of vivid memories from college golf tournaments. Most of them blend together in a mess of green and rain gear and conversion vans and long days and early workouts and cold Iowa winters. But I do have a vivid memory from this day. I will never, in my entire life, forget standing on the 18th green, waiting to tap in, and considering my options.

There were two ways that it could go.

I could walk off of the green, collapse into a mess of tears, and throw myself one heck of a self-indulgent pity party. I could wallow for hours —for days even. People would feel terrible for me. My teammates would hurt for me. My parents would call to tell me that they still loved me even though it didn't work out how I had hoped.

Or, I could take a deep breath, sincerely congratulate Stacey (my friend who was about 47 seconds away from winning) and remember that this is just a game.

I could choose happy. I could choose peace. I could choose to just let this roll off of my back.

I made a choice in that moment that dictated not only how I handled myself after that round, but how I play today, how I coach, and how I overcome other obstacles, heartbreaks and disappointments in my life.

I chose happy.

A few days after the final round of the tournament, I got an email from a man I had never met, who had been watching when I made my ten and when my round ended. He told me that even though it might be hard to imagine at the time, I would eventually be so grateful that this happened to me. And that I would learn more from making that 10 than I could have ever learned from winning.

He was completely right.

Was I upset about losing? Unbelievably. Did I cry? You bet — for an hour straight in my car on the way home.

And that's okay.

It's impossible to be happy 100% of the time on the golf course. But why not try?

Here's the secret:

If you can control your attitude, your emotions, and the way you feel about yourself on the course — you can do anything. You can shoot any score, win any tournament, but above all, you can have fun. You can actually enjoy golf. You can appreciate golf for what it is — a game.

And when you are able to come to the course every day with a positive attitude, a joyful mindset, and a commitment to giving your absolute best effort, good things will happen.

I promise you that.

All of us have our own 10 on 10. Some golf moment— a flubbed chip, lost bet, missed putt — that threatens to dull our shine and dampen our spirit. Don't let it. Choose happy. Keep reading.

_____

Olivia Lansing Herrick is a rock star on the golf course. She won 9 times during her four years at Drake, including two Missouri Valley Conference championships. She is the is the only woman to complete the "Am Slam" in Minnesota, (winning the four main amateur events in the same summer) and has won every tournament in Minnesota at least once, including the State Open. Seriously. She is also a three-time Minnesota Golf Association Women's Player of the Year (2010, 2013, 2014). And at one point, she was the 28th ranked amateur in the world. But more importantly, she is a joyful, family-loving design-aholic, with a knack for bringing out the best in people. And she once bedazzled jeans for an 'N Sync concert. Catch her smiling on the course, creating killer graphic design work for her studio (www.OliviaHerrick.com), or eating obscene amounts of rice at Big Bowl (it's basically her second home).

Chapter 1

Iced Tea and Lemonade

He had a giant smile.

But he was only a straight driver on the course.

When I was a teenager, the Burnet Senior Classic hit town to play at one of our local courses. The whole event was well done. There were clinics for kids, autograph opportunities, and ways to volunteer on the course. (Although you had to pay $50 to volunteer...but you got some sweet khaki pants).

The best part was that there was a Pro-Am the day before the official tournament began, and local kids could sign up to caddy for the "Ams."

So, my brother and I signed up.

The day of the Pro-Am, my mom dropped us off at the gates and we went to the registration desk to get our assignment. We immediately noticed the throngs of people, the well-manicured course, and the line of Lincoln Town Car courtesy cars. We later found out they were for the Pros to use.

My brother was assigned to some businessman for the day.

Me? I had a guy who worked for Denny Hecker. And Denny Hecker, Mr. Fraud himself, was in our group.

He was not a nice guy. If you don't know who he is, Google him. You won't like him either. But this story is not about him.

My group was about ten minutes away from our tee time when we made our way over to the 1st tee.

My "Ams" were Denny Hecker and his employees. And my Pro was Bruce Crampton. Fun guy to be with, but he told some of the most off-color jokes my 16 year-old ears have ever heard. There is still one that is burned into my memory that I will not tell you. And he was competitive. He was grinding all day long to win. Win what? This was a Pro-Am. I didn't get it. But this story isn't about him either.

This story is about the Pro who had the biggest gallery of the day. This story is about the Pro who talked with everyone as they approached him. This story is about the Pro who just happened to be in the group directly in front of us. This story is about one happy Pro.

This story is about Arnold Palmer.

When I crossed behind the ropes to the 1st tee, Arnold Palmer was standing not 10 feet from me with a big smile on his face. He was getting ready to hit his first shot of the day.

When his turn came, he teed his ball, and with his famous Arnie follow through, smacked it straight down the fairway.

He took off down the fairway, and his gallery followed right along.

Since this was a Pro-Am, the pace of play wasn't exactly the quickest. So, we caught up to the group ahead of us on almost every hole. And even though my Pro was playing quite seriously, the cool thing was, we could watch Arnie tee off each time.

All day long, drive after drive was straight. He didn't veer off the middle more than a foot. And all day long, he had a giant smile on his face.

After I watched one Pro smile for his entire round, and another grind out every shot, our round was over.

The Pros went their own way, and the "Ams" headed to the corporate hospitality tents for some post-round fuel.

All the caddies were invited to the tents as well. It was a cool thing for a 16 year-old kid. I ate a bunch of food and had a couple Cokes. We spent nearly an hour in the tents before my mom came to pick us up.

My mom pulled in the lot and parked. She immediately asked if we had fun. (Standard question from her, and one that I always ask my kids now). It was a question that begged us to explain more.

So I told her about Arnold Palmer.

For as long as I remember, my mom always loved Arnold Palmer. I think it was the nice guy image and the big smile. Who knows? Maybe she just liked iced tea and lemonade.

Nonetheless, she was on cloud nine that I was telling her about Arnold Palmer.

She told me to explain more about the day on the drive home, so she started up the car, and we began to leave.

On our way out, she approached a stop sign to make a right turn.

There was another car coming through the intersection who had the right of way. Mom let the car go, but as the driver was making the turn, he didn't notice my mom, and turned into her lane.

He quickly corrected himself, then slowed down to give a "Sorry, that was my fault" wave.

He glanced over with a huge smile on his face, gave the wave, and kept moving.

My mom froze.

The guy who almost hit my mom was driving a blue Lincoln Town Car.

The guy was Arnold Palmer.

Chapter 2

The Lego Mentality

I love Legos.

Pure and simple. I love them.

When I was a kid, I played with Legos every day. I built spaceships and police stations and towns and castles. There was the pirate captain, the firefighter, the mechanic, and every other occupation you could think of. Every figure had the same smiling, yellow face, but different accessories. And they were all awesome.

Now I get to enjoy Legos with my kids. The pieces are a little different. The construction is a little more sophisticated. And the figures even have different expressions on their faces now.

But here is the beauty of Legos.

There are rules. And there are no rules.

Every Lego box comes with a set of instructions. Each piece has its own designated spot. And when you're finished, your architectural achievement looks exactly like it does on the box.

What happens after?

A few days later, pieces may have fallen off. Or you've gotten just a bit bored of your creation, so you want to make something else.

And you do.

But this time, you decide to throw out the instructions and build something on your own with those same pieces. Sure, you have guidelines, but you're using your imagination to create something of your own; something that makes you happy; something you're proud of. Something awesome.

That's golf.

There are a set of guidelines. There is a general structure of how golf should be played. But there are also many pieces that you can grab from golf and make them your own. You can turn it into something that makes you happy.

Just because something comes with a set of instructions, doesn't mean it's the only way to do it.

I want you to have the Lego Mentality when you play golf.

Realize that there are people that will always play by every rule. They will follow the scientific approaches to the swing. They will believe that everything has to be in its proper place.

But that's okay. Good people can disagree.

Just remember that there are other ways to play. There are a set of instructions, but multiple uses for those instructions.

There is possibility.

Take what you know about golf, and Lego of it (worst pun on the book, guaranteed).

I give you permission to make golf your own. Build a foundation on what makes you happy.

Happy golf starts here.

This book is structured in a simple format. Each chapter contains a story, a lesson based around that story, and everyday tactics you can use immediately to build confidence and have more fun.

Every lesson is something that you can relate back to your own golf game. And since you're smart, you'll see how it applies to your life as well. Every tactic is something that the happiest golfers are doing right now when they play.

For the frustrated, embarrassed, confused, and overwhelmed golfer who wants to have some more fun on the course, this is for you.

You have permission to look at golf through a new lens. To have a Lego mentality.

Chapter 3

The Ethan Formula

When my kids were really young, I had one rule.

No kids' music in my car.

Sure, the kids could listen to music in my car, but they had to stay away from the Barney, Disney, Now Kids deathtrap.

And since they were only 2 and 3 years old, I chose the music for them.

One of my favorite bands of all time is Dawes. They have mellow folk rock albums, but can kill it live. They're personable, genuine, and darn good musicians.

So, my kids were introduced to them.

Ethan (my then-3 year-old) would listen more closely than my 2 year old daughter.

After every song on the album started, he'd ask, "Dad, what song is this?"

And after each song, I'd tell him.

The same song would play the next day, and he'd ask the same question.

I'd give the same answer.

After about a week, he started to ask for the songs by name.

"Dad, can you play Fire Away?"
"Dad, can you play A Little Bit of Everything?"
"Dad, can you play Time Spent in Los Angeles?"

Finally, Ethan got hooked on this song called How Far We've Come.

He asked for it every time we got into the car.

I'd play the song, and after only 2 lines of the song were sung, he'd ask, "Dad, can you start this song over?"

The first time was no big deal. I started it over.

Then, after 2 lines were sung again, he'd ask, "Dad, can you start this song over?"

I guess. So I did.

> 2 lines. Ask to start over.
> 2 lines. Ask to start over.

The next day, we'd get in the car again, and he'd ask to put on How Far We've Come.

This time it was different.

He listened to 4 lines of the song, and then asked, "Dad, can you start this over?"

> 4 lines. Ask to start over.
> 4 lines. Ask to start over.

I didn't understand.

Did he like the beginning of the song so much that he wanted to keep hearing it?

The pattern continued the entire week. And each time we got into the car, he listened to a few more lines of the song.

But this time, I paid attention a little more. I watched him in the rearview mirror.

And I spotted something.

I saw his little lips mouthing the words of the song, barely audible. I could see that he was right on point and then he started to mumble and fumble through a few words.

Right when the mumbling and fumbling occurred, he'd ask to start the song over.

I saw this pattern the whole car ride.

8 lines, 10 lines, half the song...

Eventually, we listened to the entire song.

The following day, we got into the car and he asked the standard question, "Dad, can you play How Far We've Come?"

We listened to the entire song straight through.

No starting over.

I was happy that he got what he wanted out of it.

But then something cool happened.

He asked a similar question, "Dad, can we listen to that again?"

And so we did.

Only this time, in a confident little 3 year old voice, he sang every word of that song for me to hear.

I learned a lot from watching my son try to figure out the words to a song. He's got a solid memory for song lyrics, but I started to understand the process at which he learned it.

It wasn't a fluke.

And I realized it's how I teach golf lessons and life lessons to my students.

Before Ethan zeroed in on How Far We've Come, we listened to the album (all 12 songs) over and over again. He could list every song on the album, but he only wanted to hear certain ones. (Post Napster kid, I guess).

He had his 4 or 5 favorites.

So, first he was introduced to it. I told him the song names. I told him the guys in the band. I told him what instruments they played. He looked at the album cover and liner notes. He couldn't read, but he liked to take things in.

Then, he started to enjoy the album. Not every song. But some of them.

Then he took baby steps to learn one song. Just one.

After he knew the lyrics to one, he'd go on to another one of his favorite songs.

He'd figure out those lyrics and move on.

Pretty soon, he knew the lyrics to about half the album. And it made him really happy. You could tell he was proud of himself. And more importantly, he liked singing the words to the songs.

The cool thing was that he started to notice the songs in public when they'd be played over the speakers. He'd sing along and get a big smile on his face.

One of the best lessons I ever learned was:

Give people what you know, and let them figure it out. Because when they figure it out, they own it. The self discovery piece is huge.

You'll read a lot of information in this book. And it's your choice what to do with it. You may choose to look and it and say, "Hmm, that's good stuff" and do nothing with it.

Or, you can do what the happy golfers do and use the tactics that you'll read.

So, did Ethan learn the song lyrics on his own? Absolutely.

Did he have some guidance along the way? Absolutely.

I didn't know what the outcome was going to be. He could love the songs or hate them. But I liked Dawes and wanted to introduce them to someone that I loved. I couldn't control the outcome, but I could control the probability.

So here's what I did (I do the same thing in my golf programs)....

1. **I helped him like something first.** I played all the songs until he hit upon a few that he really liked. Then we stuck with those.

2. **I let him learn at his own pace.** He listened to the same songs over and over again, line by line, until he finally got what he wanted. He told me when he was done.

3. **I let him make mistakes.** When he fumbled over words, I didn't tell him what those words were. He kept listening and eventually figured them out.

4. **I let him learn one thing at a time.** Sure it got annoying listening to the same 4 lines over and over again, but it's easier to master one thing first, instead of doing a bunch of things just okay. Plus, more importantly...

5. **I made it about him, not me.** He didn't care about listening to the rest of the songs. He wanted one to start. Golf is no different. Find that one thing that makes you happy. Remember, you are playing for your reasons, and for nobody else.

So take this and use it next time you play golf. This is how it will translate into golf.

1. Go out and have fun first. Make this the number one priority. It doesn't matter what your fun looks like compared to anyone else. Just make sure you enjoy what you're doing.

2. Do things at your own pace. If you want to play 1 hole, play 1 hole. If you want to just go the driving range, just go there. If you only want to putt, just putt.

3. You're going to screw up. This is inevitable. You're going to mess it up big time. You think your ball will go one way and it will go the other. You'll have awkward conversations. You'll flirt with the beverage cart girl and she'll shoot you down. You're going to screw up...and you'll be fine.

4. Tackle one thing at a time. Learn one shot. Have one conversation. Meet one new person. Learn one new rule. One thing. Master it. Move on.

5. Make golf about you. Your reasons are the most important reasons of all. As my boys in Metallica so eloquently said, "And nothing else matters."

This is the Ethan formula. Like it now, learn it later.

And it goes full circle.

Because a year after he started to like Dawes and learn the lyrics, I took him to his first concert.

Dawes at the Minnesota State Fair.

He sang. He danced. And he smiled for every minute of it.

Chapter 4

Golf Has A Giant Problem

For someone who doesn't know much about golf, the perception of the game is brutal.

And there are reasons that I hear over and over again....

"It's too intimidating."

"I'm too embarrassed."

"I wouldn't be any good."

"I don't have any clubs."

And worst of all....

"It doesn't look like it's fun."

Sound familiar? Ever said any of those things?

The outside world views golf as a bunch of old, white dudes, wasting 5 hours being frustrated. The only thing they gain is time away from the family and a bad sock tan. (Neither are exactly high on my list).

And the inside world (those of us who play golf) sometimes view it that way too. Sometimes we feel golf has too many dumb rules and too many ways to suck the fun out of the day.

Whatever happened to hanging out with some friends, having some laughs, and just playing to play?

At the 2014 PGA Merchandise Show, TaylorMade Golf announced a plan to help bring back the fun to golf. They created a site called

HackGolf.org to help gather insight into what makes golf not as fun as it could be. In layman's terms...what do you not like about golf?

The idea is that you can log on to the site and write down your thoughts, and then TaylorMade will gather the best ideas that would help make golf more fun.

The concept is great. But I realized something as I read through the comments and ideas.

Golf has a giant problem.

Let's talk through what this problem is, and what we've done about it.

Here's what would happen with other sports when I was younger...(I bet you can relate)...

My friends and I wanted to play basketball, so we grabbed a basketball and found a court. We'd pick teams and start. We made our own rules, and called our own fouls. Any amount of people could play because we'd have subs or figure out teams on our own. We goofed around, maybe kept score and had fun. And if we didn't want to play 3 on 3, or 4 on 4, we'd play HORSE. Or we'd play lightning. Or have a dunk contest (lot of short hoops in our neighborhood).

Baseball was the same way. Most of us had gloves, but if not, we shared. Usually 1 kid had a nice aluminum bat, so he'd bring that. We'd find a real baseball if we could, but if not, we'd get tennis balls, or whiffle balls. We NEVER had 18 people together at the same time, so we could never play a REAL game of baseball. At least that's what critics would say. We didn't care. We'd modify the rules to play "pitcher's hand." Or have ghost runners. And if we didn't feel like doing that, we'd have a home run hitting contest, or take grounders.

Swimming was the best of all. We found some place with open water and goofed around. We had water fights. We played water volleyball. We splashed each other. Never once when someone asked to go swimming, did we say, "Sure, I'll grab the ropes. My dad will be the timer. And we'll have a race."

See where I'm going with this?

Professional basketball games differ from pickup basketball. And professional basketball players differ from us.

Professional baseball games differ from pickup baseball. And professional baseball players differ from us.

Olympic swimming competitions differ from swimming with friends. And Olympic athletes differ from us.

Golf has too many barriers to play "pick up."

The golf purists think that we should play how the rules are written. The golf purists think that "real" golf is playing 18 holes of golf. The golf purists think that we must always keep score. The golf purists think that everyone should have their own clubs. The golf purists think that only 4 people can play together. The golf purists think that you should have a certain level of ability to play the game.

I'm not a golf purist.

I'm just a reasonable dude who wants to see people have fun.

Golf is a nearly impossible game to "pick up."

Think about how it's marketed on TV.

All you ever hear about is improving your swing and lowering your scores. The TV analysts break down every bad thing that's happening in a golf swing when that dumb little white ball is only 20 feet off from a 180 yard shot.

They are telling you how bad you are before you even start.

You didn't need a lot of skill to play other pick up games. You could learn as you played.

But golf purists will tell you that you need to have skill to play golf.

And think about it, in order to play what most people consider golf (because the purists have made it so)...

- You would need your own set of clubs.
- You would need your own bag.
- You would need your own balls.
- You would need your own tees.
- You couldn't go when you wanted. You would need to make a tee time.
- You would have to find 3 other friends who have their own set of clubs and can make it at that same tee time.

And to top it all off, you would have to pay for all of this. You can't just go and play a pick up game of golf.

Until now.

You can create your own happiness.

We did.

I have some smart people that work for me. I only hire high school and college aged kids, for a few different reasons.

First of all, they get along great with the kids in my programs. Secondly, they bring a sense of youth and possibility to the adults in my programs. And lastly, they are darn creative.

They love the games we play with the kids. And do a great job of entertaining and educating them at the same time.

Last year, we developed the greatest golf game ever created. From the beginning we knew it was good, because every group would ask to play it.

We played this with every class. Our 5 year olds. Our 8 year olds. Our middle schoolers. Our high schoolers. Our adults. Beginners. Experienced. It didn't matter.

Every single group LOVED it.

The game is a combination of capture the flag, Battleship, chess, croquet, and pool.

We call it Battleball.

And it's the game that will define pick up golf.

Why is this so important to me? Why do I stress games and fun over performance and skill.

For this reason...

Your skills will deteriorate. You will hit the ball shorter. Your scores will be higher. But what remains will be your character. And your enjoyment. And everything else you can gain from this game.

Golf has enough barriers to entry as it is. And the game has even more problems in keeping players because of the purist attitudes.

We make golf fun for you. We want to hang out with our friends and play a game.

That's Battleball. That's pick up golf. That's our kind of golf.

I'm going to show you how to create your own foundation. Your own possibility. Your own Battleball.

Chapter 5

The Magic Johnson Speech

I specifically remember walking into basketball practice in November of 1991.

Daniel Belina was eating a sugar packet (pre-5 hour Energy? - maybe he was on to something) and Magic Johnson had just announced that he had HIV.

As an 8th grader, I didn't know much about sugar packets and HIV. But I figured neither could be that good for you.

The Magic Johnson thing interested me because I didn't understand it that well and immediately he got a ton of backlash. People were saying he should quit basketball. Some players were scared they were going to get HIV from him if they played in the same game. There was a lot of naiveté, and a lot of hate.

So, I did what any 8th grader with a love of basketball (and not many friends) would do. I researched it. I wanted to know more about what HIV did, how it spread, and what the ramifications were for one of the greatest basketball players ever.

I read and read, and then I wrote.

I wrote a speech about Magic Johnson and took the side that he should not quit basketball because of HIV.

Now, normally I wouldn't just write out a speech for the fun of it, but we had a project due that required me to choose a topic, write a speech, and present it to the class.

I practiced the speech in front of the mirror at home. I read it to my parents. I tweaked it, added some parts, and made it pretty good (for an 8th grader).

The day came where it was my turn to give the speech.

I went to the front of my 8th grade class and talked for 5 minutes. Yep, just talked. I had practiced so much and knew the topic so well, that I was at ease. Sure, I was a little nervous before I went up there. But then, I just talked.

There were a lot of stunned faces in my class as my speech ended.

And it wasn't because I chose a somewhat controversial topic (at the time) to talk about.

The stunned faces of my classmates came from the fact that I actually talked.

See, I was the quiet kid. The kid who kept to himself, went about his business, and never really said much. Even on the basketball team, I kept quiet and just played.

My classmates were shocked.

And so was I.

I was scared and nervous to have a general conversation with someone, but up in front of an audience, I felt fine.

My teacher liked the speech so much that she wanted me to give it for the 7th and 8th grade assembly.

So I did. I was nervous before I walked up, but once again felt fine while talking.

Then it got a little crazy.

My 8th grade teacher told me that there was a district-wide speech competition that she recommended I go to. She said that 6th, 7th, and 8th graders from around the district would be coached in small groups and each student would present their speech in front of that group.

Then, everyone would get back together and we'd hear a few speeches picked at random.

The small groups had about 25 people each, and there was a total of about 400 parents and students.

I presented my speech for the small group. Felt fine. Then, went back to the grand assembly.

The moderator announced that she was randomly choosing three 6th graders, three 7th graders, and three 8th graders from a hat. When she said that I froze.

Now, I felt okay giving my speech in front of 25 people or so, but 400 was a whole different story.

I remember looking back at my mom who was one row behind me and saying, "If they call my name, I'm not..."

And before I could finish my sentence, I heard the moderator say, "Bryan Skavnak" (or some variation of that crazy Polish last name).

Oh man. I couldn't believe it. What the heck were the odds that my name would be called? Let alone, the very first name to be called?

I was freaking out.

There sat the quiet kid who barely made a peep before 3 weeks ago, and now I had to talk in front of 400 people.

Once again, I glanced back at my mom, and she was smiling.

She gave me this, "Go get em" look and this really weird thumbs up. Seriously, my mom was awesome at many things, but for some reason she never mastered clapping on beat or giving a normal thumbs up.

As the first name called, I was the first one to speak.

.

So I took the look and the weird thumbs with me as I walked to the podium.

I was nervous. But for 5 minutes, I just talked.

People clapped, and I walked off.

Looking back, I'm sure it wasn't the greatest of speeches. I'm sure I fumbled over some words. I'm sure I didn't give enough eye contact. I'm sure I didn't have enough charisma.

But we all have to start somewhere, right?

I was the quiet kid who just talked in front of 400 people.

Nobody pointed and laughed. Nobody booed me. And even though I probably thought people were going to judge me, they didn't.

They were too worried about themselves. And relieved when their name wasn't called.

And look what happened...

I gave speeches all through high school. I danced to Bye Bye Bye in college in front of 500 people. Yes that's an 'N SYNC song, and yes, I'm proud of it. And now, I speak to groups big and small (over 600 at my recent Junior Golf Leader award ceremony).

The quiet kid now talks for a living.

And I absolutely love it.

The point is...

You can do this.

You can do whatever you want.

You can be happy. And I can show you how.

It's nearly impossible to just have confidence. We need to build confidence.

I started with something that interested me (Magic Johnson and HIV).
I learned more about what interested me.
I organized what interested me into small parts (the speech).
I presented what interested me (this is the hardest part).
I didn't explode.
I presented again.
I didn't explode again.

Each time I didn't explode, I felt a little better about what I was doing.

Sure, it's practice. But, it's also the fact that you have to be vulnerable...and do it.

I'm going to share with you stories and tactics that you can use to build confidence, and yes, be vulnerable. You are going to answer a lot of questions that will give you a broader perspective.

There is a journey I'm going to take you on. And along this journey, you'll have to do things before you play, while you play, and after you play. Here's what we're going to do:

Step 1 - Crush Fear
Step 2 - Answer Your Big Why
Step 3 - Create Happiness Pillars
Step 4 - Explore Shots and Situations

My job is to show you how to be a happier golfer.

But more importantly, my job is to show you the possibility.

Step 1 is the most important.

Crush fear by getting out of your own way.

I believe in you. Other people believe in you. So, it's time you start believing in yourself.

I've seen a guy break 90 for the first time by shooting 76, so you can do it.

I've seen a quiet kid open up and make a bunch of friends, so you can do it.

I've seen a guy publish 2 books about happiness after his mom died, so you can do it.

One of my favorite bands in the world is Cloud Cult. They simply write great songs.

They have a song called, "You're the Only Thing in Your Way."

My favorite line in the song, "You've come too far to care what they say. Now you're the only thing in your way."

The belief, the confidence....I can help you get there. But it starts with you.

You can do this. Let's be happy together.

I may even give you a weird thumbs up.

Chapter 6

5 Words

I was scared.

My golf career started the summer before my junior year of college.

In the mornings, I worked on the grounds crew at a local golf course. And in the afternoons, I taught Park and Recreation classes to kids.

There was this girl at the course that immediately caught my eye. She was cute, had a great smile, and had a resemblance to Christina Aguilera. (Genie in Bottle Christina Aguilera, not plastic zombie Barbie Christina Aguilera).

She worked in the clubhouse and on the beverage cart, and I'd try to see her as much as I could.

My main job on the grounds crew was to cut the cups on each of the holes (and yes, the cups change every day).

But, right before lunch, I'd also have to collect all the water jugs on the course and fill them up with fresh water and ice. Bonus for me, because I'd make sure I took my sweet time filling up the water, just so I could see this girl.

I'd say hi, maybe make a little small talk, but that's about it.

See, college Bryan was a bit of a pansy.

Let's be a little more clear...

I was scared.

I don't exactly know what I was scared of...but I was scared.

Maybe it was rejection. Maybe it was saying something stupid. Maybe it was just meeting someone new.

Whatever the reason, it was way easier to just say hi everyday than to do what I really wanted to do.

I wanted to ask her out.

For many people, that seems like a no-brainer thing to do. But, for me, it was scary.

So in my head, I would start making excuses to justify my fear. "She probably has a boyfriend." "She wouldn't go out with me anyway." "I'm not good enough for her."

So, for two months during the summer I filled up water in the clubhouse and said hi. When she was driving on the beverage cart, I'd wave and say hi. And on those days when I felt it was time to man up, I wimped out.

Until one day, three weeks before I was going back to college, I finally did it.

I saw her driving down the fairway on the beverage cart. I was in my cart listening to Genie in a Bottle on my Discman. (Okay, I really wasn't listening to it, but how good would have that been...and remember Discmans?)

She pulled up next to me as she usually did when we saw each other on the course, so we could chat for a bit.

I was nervous and I didn't know why. Come on, I was 21 and for 2 months I couldn't ask this girl out? What the heck was wrong with me?

I summoned the courage, fumbled over my words, and asked her.

"Do you want to go out sometime?"

Not articulate. Not overly thought out (you'd think it would have been after 2 months).

She put her hands on her hips, smiled at me, and then spoke.

And her response floored me.

She said 5 words.

"What took you so long?"

You want an instant confidence boost? Have a cute girl that you're too afraid to ask out say those 5 words to you. Have anybody you know say that to you. Heck, say it to yourself.

What took you so long?

We dated for a month and I went back to college. The long distance thing didn't work, so we went our separate ways. But it was fun for a month.

Our lives are made up of far too many, "What took you so longs?"

We linger. We wait. We see our chance fly by. Our genie goes back in the bottle.

Fear stops us. Fear controls us. But it doesn't have to.

Golf. Life. Relationships. They are no different.

We need to take the steps to crush our fear and be happy.

It's starts with a choice.

Chapter 7

Reality of Rejection

Choices don't need to be rights or wrongs. Choices can just be choices.

Because choosing is always better than lingering.

Choosing is better than waiting around for someone to choose for you.

Sure, I'd love if you implemented everything in this book.

Why? Because I know it works.

I've seen it in action. I've tested. I've gotten results.

But I realize that most people won't do it all...if anything.

We get stuck listening to concepts and educating ourselves, but we forget the most important thing.

Implementing.

If we just took a step back for a second and made the decision to actually do something, to start something, then our lives would be totally changed.

But, we either get lazy or make excuses, or most of all...we get scared.

Fear stops us.

Because it's the fear of the unknown.

It's the fear of "what if it's not good?"

It's the fear of "what if other people don't like it?"

But really, it's the fear of rejection.

We are all scared.

We are scared of failing. We are scared of rejection. We are scared of looking stupid. But, in reality, we are just really bad at math.

I have many people that have helped me out in various parts of my life. One of those people is a guy named Brendon Burchard. He speaks all over the world. He trains some of the biggest companies. And he told a story once that completely changed how I view things. Straight up, changed my life.

It was a story about the reality of rejection. And how we are all scared to be rejected.

It went like this....

Think for a minute about a time in your life when you felt that someone rejected you. A time where it really hit home, it really hurt. It put a dent in you. It affected how you did things. It could be a break up. It could be an idea that wasn't taken. It could be a job. It could be someone just being unkind to you.

Would you say this has happened to you once in your life?

Of course. Most people have had a person in their lives that have rejected them and hurt them.

Let's think about it again. Has this happened to you more than once? Someone that has really hurt you. Someone that doesn't want you, that doesn't like what you do. Someone that has hurt the core of who you are. Someone who has told you you're not good enough. Not smart enough. Not ready enough.

Can you think of three people in your life that have rejected you?

Sure. It might be a struggle, but yes, you can probably think of three people.

So, again. Think about it. Have you been rejected by five people that have really hurt how you feel about yourself and your identity?

Possibly.

Have you been rejected by 7 people?

Maybe.

How about 10 people?

Less likely.

20 people?

Probably not.

Brendon has asked this question all over the world. The average in his seminars is about 7 people. So, in each of our lives, there have been about 7 people that don't like us or what we do. 7 people who have rejected us.

Now think about this.

Have you had people in your life that you've met, interacted with, spent time with, networked with, and it's seemed to go pretty well?

Can you think of 20 people?

Can you think of 50 people?

Have you met people in your life that are fine with what you're doing? That have been cool with you.

In your whole life, have you met 200 people like that?

500 people? 1,000 people?

If you really sit back and think about it, you could come up with a pretty big list of people that you've met with, spent time with, talked with...and it went just fine.

So, we've been rejected 7 times in our life. And we have met 1,000 people that are cool with us.

Yet, we make a crucial mistake.

We let those 7 people run our lives.

We think about the rejection that may happen. We don't take risks. We don't put ourselves out there. We don't try something we want to do.

Why?

Because we're scared of 7 people.

7 people!

We're letting 7 people dictate what we should do.

We're worried about what 7 people think? We're not being ourselves, following our dreams, doing something that makes us happy because of 7 people?

7 people or 1,000 people.

Rejection rarely happens. We just suck at math.

We've got 1,000 people in our corner who are cool with us. We've got 1,000 people who support us. And 7 people who judge us.

Screw the 7. Let's make the 1,000 people happy.

Think about if you were driving to work and just tried to avoid all the potholes. You'd be swerving all over. You'd be off the road.

Think about if you got up to a tee box on the golf course and instead of trying to hit it down the fairway, you just tried NOT to hit it in the water.

When I walk up the stairs, I don't try NOT to trip. I just walk.

We think rejection happens all the time. But the reality is, rejection rarely happens.

Our 1,000 supporters could stomp those 7. They would crush those 7.

You have 1,000. I have 1,000. We have people that like us. We have people that care about us. We have people that are happy to know us.

Don't live your life for the 7. Live your life for the 1,000.

And most of all, live your life for yourself.

Decide what to be and go be it.

Go be happy.

Chapter 8

Scorecard Fear

So how does this fear stuff relate to golf? What is it about golf that makes us so scared?

Most of us don't even know that we are scared of something in golf. But we are. It's happened to me. I've seen it in thousands of my students.

We have Scorecard Fear.

Scorecard Fear is when the fear of getting a high number or a high score drives you to feel nervous, anxious, angry, and frustrated. You think too far in advance of your score. You play scared golf. You try to guide your ball instead of focusing on the target.

In high school, I took golf a little too seriously and got mad when I didn't do well. In college, I realized that I didn't do well at times because I was scared. I was scared of how I played, what other people would see in me, and I didn't want to be embarrassed. I had Scorecard Fear.

I let a dumb number on a piece of paper control how I played. I was too concerned with the outcome.

You can't control outcomes, only probabilities.

What does that mean?

It means that you don't know how things will end up. So, no need to focus on a perfect outcome. Instead, do something to help the outcome. Give yourself a chance.

The reason we have scorecard fear isn't that we are embarrassed about a high number. It goes deeper. We believe that somehow the high number is a reflection on our character. That we are not good enough.

You can watch the Golf Channel, read Golf Digest, and take lessons that focus strictly on lowering your score. But eventually that learned skill deteriorates. Eventually, you're just not as good as you used to be.

But you still have character. You still have your values.

It doesn't matter if you win any golf tournaments.
It doesn't matter if your score goes down.
It doesn't matter if you beat everyone in your group.
It doesn't matter if you have a bunch of trophies.
It doesn't matter if your swing is flawless.

What matters is that you really enjoy doing something. What matters is who you are. What matters is your character.

When kids come back year after year, I like seeing how they have grown. Not in size, or stature, or golf ability, but in terms of character.

Are they getting along with their sister better?
Are they doing better in school?
Are they appreciating what their parents do for them?
Are they trying their best?
Are they trying to make other people feel good?
Are they being generous?

That stuff matters.

I'm very lucky to be in a position that can influence kids and help them become more confident, happy adults.

And I'm lucky that I have some great kids in my program.

There's a kid in one of my classes...let's call him Charlie (because that's his name).

Charlie is a great kid. He gets along with other kids in the class. He's smart. He's a hard worker. He loves trying trick shots I show him. And yeah, he's a good golfer.

At Christmastime, I sent Charlie a t-shirt that said, "I'd rather be golfing with Bryan."

We'd always gotten along great, and I thought he'd get a kick out of it.

A week later, I got a package in the mail.

It was the same style envelope that I had sent him.

I opened it up and pulled out a bright pink t-shirt.

It said, "I'd rather be golfing with Charlie."

Charlie is a good golfer. But he's a better person.

Chapter 9

Tension

When I first started teaching, my mentor would sit me down between lessons and make me watch.

We'd watch the driving range and all the people on it.

It was usually filled with a few avid golfers, a few families, a few beginners, and a few people who you knew watched the Golf Channel last night.

We'd watch their swing and their movements, but most of all we'd watch for tension.

The way golf is taught and the way golf is played makes it a dominant force for tension. And most of it is unwarranted tension.

The avid golfers would be tense from not hitting a perfect shot.

The families would be tense with dad and mom telling the kids how to swing.

The beginners would be tense with the embarrassment they felt from not doing as well as everyone else.

The Golf Channelers would be tense because they had 12,000 thoughts in their heads.

Do you do many things well when you are tense?

I sure don't. And I don't know many people that do.

Break it down to really simple terms for a second...

You are tense about golf.

About golf?!

You didn't lose your house. You didn't lose your job. You didn't get into an accident. Nobody around you died.

You are tense about not hitting a stupid little white ball to a hole in the ground 100 yards away.

I think we need to reexamine what's important.

Just because you haven't yet figured out how to make the golf ball do what you want it to do, doesn't make you a bad person. It doesn't make you a failure. It doesn't make you a loser.

It makes you a person.

You will never be satisfied with golf until you understand why you are playing golf.

Everyone is taught to perfect their swing and lower their score.

What about the rest of golf?

Shouldn't the avid golfer be happy that they get a little freedom from the office for the afternoon?

Shouldn't the families be happy with spending time together playing a game and building their relationships with each other?

Shouldn't the beginner be happy that they have a new challenge in their life?

Shouldn't the Golf Channelers be happy that they are taking risks and willing to make a change?

Golf is not swing and score.

Golf is personal.

And I realize that you have some tension right now with this whole golf thing.

Make it personal for you. Don't let the golfing world push you into thinking that swing and score is all that matters.

Because people matter too.

I had my wake up call (literally) a few years ago.

Read on.

Chapter 10

The Night

I was sitting by myself.

Even though I was surrounded by my dad, my brother, my wife, my aunts and my uncles, I was still by myself.

And I was thinking.

7 months earlier on Halloween night 2010, I got a phone call.

I was sleeping. It rang again and woke me up. The caller ID showed mom and dad.

I knew this couldn't be good.

It was my dad on the line.

"Bryan, your mom is really sick. The ambulance is coming to take her to the E.R."

My mom never complained about being in pain or being sick. So, when my dad calls me to let me know, I better listen.

At any other time, my dad would have taken my mom himself. But he just had a full left hip replacement...for the third time. Dude is bionic.

"What do you want me to do?," I asked.

"Nothing right now. But hold on the line a second, I think the EMT is here."

Then out of nowhere, I heard my mom screaming.

That is not a sound I wish on anyone.

But the weird thing was that she wasn't screaming out of pain.

She kept saying, "Are you all right Johnny? Are you all right Johnny?"

I didn't know what was going on.

I just kept listening.

About 30 seconds later, a guy got on the phone. It was the EMT.

"Hello?"

"Yes, is this their son?"

"Yes," I said.

"I have a bit of a situation here. Your mom is having severe abdominal pain. And your dad just fell down the stairs."

Silence.

I didn't even know what to say.

I didn't know if he was badly hurt, unconscious, or what.

"Let me call you back in 20 minutes," he said.

That was the worst 20 minutes of my life.

He called back and told me that both my parents were headed to the E.R.

So I met them there.

My mom always told me look on the bright side. So if there was any bright side to this, they made it convenient for me. They were in adjacent E.R. rooms, so I could just pop in one and then back to the other one.

Apparently, when my dad heard the EMT come to the door, he was hobbling around on his crutches, trying to maneuver their split level home. His crutch got caught in the carpet at the top of the steps, and he went tumbling down the stairs onto the tile floor.

Miraculously, my dad came out of it with just a bruise. A giant bruise, but just a bruise.

My mom?...

That was the night she was diagnosed with lymphoma.

So, 7 months after "The Night," I was sitting by myself in a chair in a hospital room. Remembering.

It was in that chair, in that hospital, waiting out the inevitable, that my life changed.

Because when I was sitting in the hospital room, waiting out her last few days, something weird happened.

I remembered everything.

My dad, my brother, my wife, my aunts and my uncles...we started talking about mom. All the good times, all the funny times, all the sad times. We just talked. We shared story after story. We cried a little and we laughed a lot.

And it hit me.

This is life.

Relationships, stories, connections, memories, people. That's life.

Life is not about stuff. Golf is not about score.

You can have the houses and cars and toys and gadgets.

I want the people. People matter.

It's about your family, your friends, and your stories.

Sometimes it takes a difficult time in your life to realize what you really want.

Sometimes it's just making a choice.

On that day, my life changed because I made a choice to change it.

I no longer wanted to be the golf pro that showed you how to hit a straight shot in the air or make a 10 foot putt.

I wanted to be more.

I wanted to show you what golf can do for you.

And pass it all on.

I had always taught golf to be fun. I had always made golf a break from the rest of your life. I had always made golf less serious than everyone else seemed to be making it.

But, I never told you why.

It was in that corner chair of the hospital room, where my mom was about to die, that I decided to start telling my "Why."

Chapter 11

The Letter

You may have seen this letter before. But it's worth sharing again. Because this letter is what started it for me. This is the beginning of my "Why." I wrote this letter one week after my mom died. I didn't know what to expect, but I wrote it anyway and sent it out to all my students.

I lost my number one fan last week.

After battling lymphoma for seven tough months, my mom died on Tuesday.

She was the happiest person you'd ever meet. She would talk your face off. When I was growing up, some people even thought that I was mute because I could never get a word in.

She was pro-family all the way...dinners together, holidays together, anything you could think of....together.

She started to learn how to golf because it was a fun family thing to do. She was never very good, but she had fun with it.

My mom was the one who asked religiously every time I came home, if I got a hole in one. She only forgot to ask once. And I had to remind her...because that's the day I got a hole in one.

My mom was the one who'd walk along with me and root me on during my playing days, even when she couldn't see where the ball went. I remember a time at a Monticello tournament, where I ripped two out of bounds, and she said, "Nice shot BR."

My mom was the one who would say to me, "Don't worry Bryan, I don't tell anyone you tried to teach me...you'll lose business if I do!"

You always learn a lot from people you're the closest to. Some things are specifically taught and others you just pick up along the way.

My mom taught me about manners, and generosity, and treating others kindly. She taught me how to play 500 (she was a rockstar at that game), how to make ice cream pie, and how to do laundry. She taught me how to pray, how to talk to others, and how to sing incorrect song lyrics. Seriously, I still don't know what a heebeejeebee is.

She taught me it's okay to laugh and it's okay to cry.

But the greatest gift my mom ever gave me was perspective.

It was the realization that you can be happy if you choose to be happy. It was the fact that no matter how bad you have it, someone else has it worse. It was not knowing all the answers, but always looking for ways to make things better. It was perpetual positivity.

There is no glass half empty or glass half full. There is just a glass, and you put what you want into it.

My mom was happy until the end. She never complained, never wondered why this happened to her, and through it all worried about how we were doing.

It takes a special person to stay positive through tough times. Although it takes a very special person to talk to a wrong number for 20 minutes (she had done that before too!).

I'll leave you with my favorite mom story ever. It was just between us two and I've never laughed so hard in my life. To my friends, it's simply known as Peanut Butter Chocolate Chip.

We were shopping at Brookdale in the winter. We parked near Sears and had to walk through it to get to the mall. On the way out, I saw someone who worked there that I knew, and didn't feel like talking to at the time.

I looked at my mom and said, "Okay, how are we going to do this?"

Without hesitation, my mom said, "We need code words." I almost lost it right there.

My mom saying, "we need code words" was the equivalent to me saying, "No thanks, I don't want any more cake." You never saw it coming.

So we came up with a plan.

I was going to weave through the store, Frogger-style, with my mom shouting "code words" when I should go left or right. In retrospect, I could have taken a different door out, but this was way more fun.

"Okay mom, what are the code words?"

"If you should go left, I'll say chocolate chip.

"And what if I need to go right?"

"Peanut butter."

So, the plan began.

I started walking through an aisle and all of a sudden heard my mom screaming, "Peanut butter!, Peanut butter!, Peanut butter!"

I went to the right and walked DIRECTLY in front of the person I did not want to talk to.

But I was okay, because he never saw me. He was too busy staring at this crazy woman yelling "Peanut butter" in the middle of Sears.

We got to the exit and we both stopped. We were laughing hysterically at this point. My mom looked at me and said, "Where were you going? I said peanut butter and you went chocolate chip."

"No. Peanut butter is right, chocolate chip is left."

By this time, people were staring at us because I think we were hyperventilating near the doors.

We walked out to the parking lot and I started going the wrong way. My mom looked at me and deadpanned, "Hey BR, the car is to the peanut butter."

Until the very end, my mom still thought peanut butter was to the left.

It's okay to laugh and it's okay to cry.

I hope you find your Peanut Butter Chocolate Chip. And remember, perspective is everything. Thanks Mom.

Chapter 12

Is This A Game Or An Event?

I teach golf to help people become happier.

That's my why.

Teaching you to get better at golf is just a small part of what I do. I also teach you to be more self confident. I teach you how to enjoy your day more. I teach you about perspective. I teach you that there is much more to golf than a swing and a score.

Because a better swing doesn't keep you playing. A better experience does.

Happy Golfers do things differently. They don't put the emphasis on swing and score.

Your job is not to learn every little thing that golf is about. Your job is not to learn the perfect swing. Your job is not to learn every rule. And most of all, your job is not to control the outcome.

Because you can't.

Give yourself the best chance at your goal, whatever that goal may be.

Let's build a foundation.

Your foundation will include questions you need to answer. Your foundation will include things you can do before you play, while you play, and after you play that will give you what you need to succeed in golf. Because your success will be based on what you want, not what other people say is acceptable.

I challenge you to think differently and act differently.

And I'll show you how.

Last year, I was at a Super Bowl party.

The party had all the essentials: a ton of food, a stocked fridge, big TVs showing the game, a bunch of friends, and White Castle (I guess that's food.....or at least I think it is).

I was in the kitchen eating my 6th slider when my friend Todd asked me a question.

"Hey Bryan, is this a game or an event?"

I'm sure I threw out some smart aleck answer. Kind of my M.O. But then it got me thinking (I know, dangerous).

I'm not a huge football fan. I don't set aside every Sunday to watch it. But if it's on at a restaurant, I'll check it out. I got kicked out of Fantasy Football the only year I played because I never paid attention and didn't make any roster moves. I understand the appeal and I see why other people love it. I'd just rather be doing something else.

But the Super Bowl party...I'd never miss it.

Why?

Because I wasn't there for the game. I was there for everything surrounding the game.

That football game is an excuse to have an event.

It's an excuse to get friends together, eat a bunch of food, make some jokes, play some games, and talk with people. I love THAT stuff.

It's the reason card clubs are formed. It's the reason bowling leagues meet. It's the reason kids get into sports.

The game is the excuse for the event.

When I take my kids to Target Field, they don't go to see if the Twins win. They go to eat popcorn and hot dogs (and whatever else their mom usually doesn't allow them to eat). They go to sing along to the music between innings. They go to see TC ride around the field.

Golf is an excuse to be with your friends. Golf is an excuse to have a duck race. Golf is an excuse to have The Daddy Caddy. Golf is an excuse to have a Skav-enger Hunt. Golf is an excuse to have a putting race. Golf is an excuse to smile, and laugh, and play.

Is showing you how to shoot a low score on the top of the list?

Absolutely not.

Showing you how to have more fun with your friends. Showing you how to LOVE doing something. Showing you how to be a part of a team. Showing you that you are better than you think you are. Those things are way up on the list.

Games are excuses to have events.

I try to make every one of my programs an event. Something that you will remember. Something that puts a smile on your face, makes you feel a little happier, and helps you.

Lessons alone won't keep people playing. Experiences keep people playing.

Sure, everything tends to be more fun when you are a little better at it. But the swing and the score is just a very small fraction of why people play the game.

More importantly, figuring out what we want out of the experience and why we play the game is a vital step in building our foundation.

What I've realized is that in order to make our experience the best one it can be, we need to answer three questions.

These are the drivers of everything we do around golf.

I call this the Why Trifecta.

The Why Trifecta

#1 - Why do you play golf?
This is the general question. What brings you out? What keeps you playing? Why do you want to try it? What interests you about it? The answer will be a big picture answer. Keep it basic. You should have multiple answers to this question.

#2 - Why do you play golf with certain people?
There are people you will want to play golf with. Who are they? And why do you play with them? When you choose certain people to play golf with, why specifically have you chosen them? Are they good friends that you can talk with on the course? Are you trying to get a business deal done? Did you enter a tournament to play competitively? Why do you choose specific people to play golf with you?

#3 - Why are you playing golf today?
This is the question we usually forget to answer. We answer #1 for the big picture, but we forget that each day we play golf may have a different meaning. Sometimes we play golf with friends we haven't seen for a while just to get together. Sometimes we play golf in a tournament. Sometimes we play golf for a bachelor party. Sometimes we play golf to impress our in-laws. Each day you play means something different. Yes, your big picture answer will guide you, but make sure you know why you are out playing golf today.

Many of you have told me why you play. "To be with friends", "to get some exercise", "to be with my kids", "for personal challenge", "to try something new"...the list goes on and on. Very rarely is the answer "to score low" or "have a great swing."

The overall experience of golf is most important factor.

If you don't have fun doing something, you won't do it anymore. I've seen really good golfers get burned out and quit. And I've seen the least talented players absolutely love the game.

The Why Trifecta is what you get from the game. Your benefits.

Do you know the top reasons 70% of kids quit sports before they're 13?

1. It's not fun.
2. Their friends don't play.

This is why I preach about forming golf teams. This is why I have a duck race. This is why I have The Daddy Caddy. This is why our 10am classes start about 10:08am. (My little secret...it's not because we're running late...it's so you can talk with other moms, dads, and kids. So you can catch up, plan play dates after golf, and tell some stories).

At the end of the day, my kids don't say, "Dad, I had a perfect swing today and made great contact."

No. They say, "That was so fun. I hit the golf ball picker, won a Jolly Rancher sucker, and stacked two golf balls on top of each other!"

Better swings and better scores will not correlate to you playing more.

Creating a better overall experience will.

Stop right now and answer the Why Trifecta.

Chapter 13

The Un-Happiest Golfers

I will totally admit when I'm wrong.

I'm wrong a lot of the time.

This was not one of those times.

Last summer, we took two of our boys' classes to a local course called Shamrock, to play on a big course.

"The Rock" is a wide open course, with some giant pine trees, and a wide variety of clientele. They cater everyone from seniors to juniors...and it's a good course for people who don't play a lot.

The plan was to take our first class on the front nine, and when they finished, the other class would take their place and play the back nine.

The plan went smoothly...except for one thing.

We got stuck behind a group that was playing really, really (yeah, 2 reallys) slow.

Our front nine of what should have lasted about an hour and 45 minutes, instead crept to about 2:10. Not terrible, but I always work with my students to play faster because it benefits everyone.

The front nine ended and we got our second class rolling to the back nine.

I was inside the clubhouse when a guy and his wife (who I quickly found out were behind my last group on the front nine) came in and started complaining to the girl working behind the desk.

The following is paraphrased...except for 2 words. You'll know which 2.

Guy: "What the heck is in front of me? Is this a lesson? There are a bunch of juniors playing slow."

Me: "Yeah, it's my group. We're actually playing pretty fast. We got stuck behind 4 people that were slowing us down too."

Girl behind desk: "Yep, it's that foursome. I've got the ranger on it to speed them up."

Guy: "No, I don't think so. These juniors are playing too slow. We shouldn't have to play behind them."

Me: "Sir, it's not us. We played the front in a little over 2 hours and would have played faster if it wasn't for that group."

This guy kept coming at me.

Guy: "These juniors are slow and shouldn't be here. And now I have to wait on the 10th for 2 more groups to go through."

Me: "No you don't. All the groups have teed off the back nine. Go look. I'd appreciate it if you dropped the attitude."

Guy's wife: "F****k you"

Whoa.

I was with one of my other instructors and we did the only thing that we could think of...

We laughed and walked away.

Sure, I wanted to say...

"You're just mad a 13 year old beat you." or "What time are you due back at the hospital?" or "Sorry you had to marry her."

But I didn't.

I laughed and walked away.

Because nothing good was going to come from me retaliating.

This was a golf course. This is where people should be enjoying the day, having fun with people they like, and relaxing.

These people probably weren't mad at me.

They probably weren't mad at my players.

They probably weren't even mad that they were playing slow.

Something else was going on, and it carried over to the golf course. I see it all the time when people take lessons.

A tough day at work = frustration with golf (if you let work carry over to golf)

A fight with a friend = frustration with golf (if you let the fight carry over to golf)

Stress at home = frustration with golf (if you let the stress carry over to golf)

If you know the reasons why you are playing, then you shouldn't be mad at your golf game. You should be enjoying the reasons you're out there in the first place.

If you were that good, you'd be on TV.

Be happy that you're playing.

Be happy that you're with people you like to be around.

And most of all, be happy that you're not married to the lady with the sailor mouth.

Chapter 14

Baseball and Blake

My 8th grade baseball coach got fired.

And he was a volunteer.

Now, how the heck does a guy who volunteers his time to work with kids, get fired?

Looking back, I believe it's because he focused too much on winning.

But this is also how...

1. Since there was snow on the field, our first practice was in a library conference room...where we took ground balls.

2. Our second practice took place the next day, on that same field...after we shoveled off the snow.

3. We had signs to learn (not uncommon) when we were batting (steal, hit and run, etc). We had to memorize a full sheet of paper filled with 19 different signs.

4. I pitched nearly every game (even though the rules said I shouldn't have), threw nearly every batting practice, then tore a tendon in my elbow.

5. He was verbally abusive when we lost...and we didn't even lose that often.

Now, I get it. There are different coaching styles. There are some people that will win at all costs. And some people believe if you are playing in a competitive league, then you should always try to win.

I'm not that guy.

Plus, this was a house league.

This was a league where we signed up with friends to PLAY baseball.

Nobody on that team ever had any illusions that we were going to play in the Major Leagues. And the sad part was that because of the coaching, some kids quit baseball and never played again.

Some golf coaches do the same thing. We try to teach the professional's swing to you. But most of us will never be on the PGA Tour, so why do some people teach that way? It doesn't make sense.

We need to look at these things differently.

We need to get past the coaching to win mentality.

We need to focus on coaching to teach; coaching to grow; and coaching for fun.

I've coached a high school girls team for 8 years.

The high school is one of the most academically intense college prep schools in Minnesota. I fell into the job by teaching one of the assistant coaches at the time. I knew nothing of the school, but thought it would be fun to coach high school level kids.

I quickly found out that there was a strong culture of high performance at the school. Not a bad thing at all. But, man, these kids had to work hard. They would consistently have 3-4 hours of homework each night, be expected to participate in athletics and other activities. Plus, the sports teams were expected to compete with the best and win state titles.

And the main focus was always keeping a top level east coast school on their radar. The goal, most definitely, was to be accepted into an excellent college.

I struggled through the first few years of coaching.

The girls didn't seem dedicated. They would skip practice. When they did practice, they seemed rushed and unfocused. They were always stressed about something and never seemed to be having any fun.

I soon realized that golf was not high on their list of priorities. They were worrying academics, and ACTs, and SATs, and projects, and studying, that golf had to take a back seat.

So I did what any other coach at an institution that valued high level performance would do.

Wait, no I didn't.

I did the opposite.

After talking with the team and figuring out why they came out for golf in the first place, I changed the focus of our team. I allowed golf to be the break from all the other things going on in the girls' lives. Every match was just time spent with friends.

Winning mentality? Depends on how you define winning.

I've always like to do the opposite.

When everyone in my 6th grade class was listening to Van Halen, I listened to New Kids on the Block. (I still remember a girl in my class saying, "Boys don't listen to that.")

When my college friends wanted to take me out for my 21st birthday to get hammered, I told them I had to study for a test. (Really, I did).

And when my governing board (The PGA) tells me that I should probably teach a certain way, I don't. I do what benefits you instead.

Golf was the outlet. At practice, we sat down, ate a bunch of food, and talked. Just talked. During matches, I started writing phrases on their golf balls to make them laugh. We didn't focus on winning. We just focused on playing.

We didn't have structured meetings or banquets. The girls just hung out, laughed, and had fun.

And to this day, that's what we still do.

We have enough to worry about in our lives. Golf is not something we need to get stressed about. Golf can be an outlet for you too. It's a chance to be with people you care about and just play a game.

We need a new approach to this game. We can't continue to focus on the superficial parts of the game. Score, swing, winning...does that really matter more than the connections and memories we can make?

Something needs to change.

And I'm here to show you that things can be different.

Sure I use golf as my backdrop to spend more time with family and have real connections with people. But, this can go for any activity. As long as you focus on the right things.

See, back 20-25 years ago, kids played in sports for fun and recreation. To get a little exercise and be with their friends.

Now, sports are overly controlled. Travel leagues dominate...and if you don't have the proper skill to play, you either drop down to a different league or you don't get to play at all.

We've forgotten the answers to our "Why" questions.

We need to get back to the times when games were fun for the players. So the parents and siblings can cheer on without worrying about getting into a fight with another dad. So the umps and referees stop taking so much abuse. We need to put winning on the back-burner and help these kids develop by playing the game, learning the game, and making mistakes.

We need to be together with the people who are important to us.

We need to be leaders.

And it all starts by answering the question, "Why?"

Once we answer the Why Trifecta, our target becomes much clearer.

Chapter 15

The Happiness Pillars

You've answered the most important questions: The Why Trifecta?

1. Why do you play golf?
2. Why do you play golf with certain people?
3. Why are you playing golf today?

This will help us form a target. Simply put, your target is your why. Your target is what makes you the happiest while playing golf. Your target is what you strive for every time you play.

We tend to lose our target sometimes because we don't have a clear idea of why we're playing in the first place. But now you have that target and that reason.

The Happiness Pillars are the things that you create and choose to make golf your own. They are the things that support your target. Remember, don't let golf mold you into something you don't want to be. You create it.

Think of it this way, if you could build golf into something that makes you happy, what would it look like?

Let's dive into the 4 Happiness Pillars.

1. Your Dream Group
2. The Game
3. The Location
4. The Scorecard

Happiness Pillar #1: Your Dream Group

A few years ago I was giving a lesson to the mom of one of my younger students. The daughter was in one of my camps a while back, and she had decided to try out for her high school golf team (because she loved the social aspect).

After a few minutes of getting caught up, I asked the mom, "So what brought you here? Why do you want to play golf?"

Without any hesitation, she said, "I'm not concerned with hitting the ball in the air. I don't want to keep score when I play. I don't even care if I'm any good. I just want to do something with my daughter."

That is a perfect why.

We all wish we could spend more time with the people we care about.

Let's build that. Let's choose the people we want to be with.

So, who is in your dream group?

Who are the 3-4 people in your life that matter most? These people are your favorite people in the world. They are the ones who you feel the best around. They challenge you and make you smile. They support you and encourage you. They make you feel better. They make you laugh.

You can be yourself around them with no judgment. You are able to have real conversations with them. Who are those people?

One of the keys to life is surrounding yourself with good people. People that support and care about you.

I ask the dream group question, because for so long, us "all knowing" golf pros have failed to realize what ultimately drives a person. We have taught what WE think needs to be taught. Usually this involves mechanics and complex movements. We have been told that teaching the student how to hit the ball further and straighter will make them love golf more.

False.

What makes one person happy may not even be on the radar of another person. Hitting the ball further and straighter may be way down on your list when you play. Maybe you just want to gain some self confidence. Maybe you just want an hour with your family.

Your Dream Group is an important choice you'll have to make.

I ask for 3-4 people because usually that's how many people are in a golf group. But really, if you have 12 important people, that's awesome. Your pillar is stronger.

And because you can have sub-Dream Groups. These sub groups are just other groups that make you happy in different ways.

Sometimes I like golfing with my wife and kids. Sometimes I like golfing with my brother and dad. Sometimes I like golfing with the girls on my team. Sometimes I like to play in tournaments.

Sometimes you'll like to be more competitive. Sometimes you'll only want to play a few holes. Sometimes you'll want to be strictly social.

Different people will fit into those criteria better. Sometimes your competitive friends and your social friends don't mix too well. That's okay. Dream Group and Sub-Dream Group. Different criteria for different groups.

When I was younger, my friends and I played to play. And we played to have fun.

All throughout the year, my friends and I would goof around and make up games. We played tackle basketball in the snow in the winter. We had tennis tournaments with Wimbledon style bracketing. We played whiffle ball in the yard until holes formed where the bases were.

I wasn't the most athletic on any of my teams, although I was the most athletic in our family. But, saying that I was the "most athletic Skavnak" is like saying Khloe is the "smartest Kardashian". Just doesn't mean much.

But I was part of something fun. So. Much. Fun.

Because even though my friends and I had varying degrees of skill, we had fun together. The skill involved didn't drive us to be together. The fact that we enjoyed being with each other laughing and competing and goofing around mattered most.

This was my Dream Group.

Now that I'm a little older, those are the fun memories I look back on. I'm sure at the time, I wanted to win every game, hit tons of home-runs, and score tons of points.

But now I know that the team mattered most. And everything surrounding the team was way more important than winning and losing.

Happiness is not in winning. Happiness is in people.

Professor Bryan

Professor Bryan.

No, I didn't make them call me that.

My first year out of college, when I was 23, I had a sweet job. I taught at the University of Minnesota.

I taught general rec golf classes through the kinesiology department. It was part of a bigger program called Golf for Business and Life.

Craziest part?

They let me give grades.

But this is not a story about that.

This is about the people in that class.

There were juniors, seniors, and grad students. There was the T.A., the cute girl, the girl who knew my brother, and the dude who always had a Coke bottle. There was a kid I went to high school with, and the girl who didn't realize she was left handed (that's a story in itself).

And even though these people came from different backgrounds, different cities, and different families, they were the same.

They wanted to have fun.

Each one of them may have signed up for the class for their own reason: fulfill a requirement, add a credit, do something with their friends, or actually learn about golf.

But once class started, having fun needed to take center stage.

Some of the fun was from games that I created.

But most of the fun came from the collection of cool people doing something together.

Because we all brought something different to the table.

The T.A. gave us perspective. He was a Sports Management Major from Korea and an exceptional Taekwondo instructor. And one of my favorite people in the world.

Mr. Coke Bottle gave us energy. He was always up beat, talkative, and ready to have fun. Part of that may have been the fact that the Coke bottle was not filled with just Coke.

Me?

I was just a guy who had gone through college before and navigated what they were trying to do now.

I had knowledge in something that I wanted to share.

Whether they were going to play golf all their lives or not didn't matter, because the knowledge I wanted to share wasn't about golf.

It was about community.

Sure golf was the stage, but the people in that class were way more important than the game.

So, I tried to bring people together by making them comfortable in this new setting. And they in turn tried to do the same by going out after class, doing college kid stuff, and spending time together. And they even let their professor join in the fun. (Can't beat a pitcher of beer and a pitcher of wings).

But, how do I know that this golf class actually did what it was supposed to do? Use golf as the stage to bring people together.

Because I still hear from the T.A. He's back in Korea now, married, with a little boy. Still teaching Taekwondo, and yes, still one of my favorite people in the world.

The cute girl, the girl who knew my brother, and my high school friend? We still talk over email and Facebook.

And the Coke bottle guy?

He's one of my good buddies. He's married with a little girl (who thank God looks more like mom). Plus, he made me a killer german chocolate cake for my b-day once.

Golf is not a white ball, some clubs, and a swing.

It's friends. It's community. It's a group of people that can do something fun together.

It's a foundation of people that can be built at any time in your life.

They may not golf.

But they are your friends. And they are your family.

They are your Dream Group.

Chapter 16

Happiness Pillar #2: The Game

Bonding Over A Game

During my freshman year of college, I went through a rite of passage.

Oh, I know what you're thinking...it wasn't that. Whoa, it wasn't that either. Come on, this is a family show.

I went through that other rite of passage.

Learning to live with a random roommate.

You may have done this before too. You were expected to live in a 10x10 room, with someone you've never met before, in a new environment, at a new place.

But I was lucky. I got matched up with a rock star. (Or, as much as an Eagle Scout can be a rock star).

See, this roommate of mine had some very redeeming qualities.

He was easy going, he was smart, and he played golf.

But the best quality of all...

He sucked at cribbage.

Now, you would think that by the title of this story, that the game in "bonding over a game" would have been golf.

Nope, it was cribbage.

I know, I know...we couldn't keep the ladies away.

We played cribbage every chance we got. Between classes, at night, while we should have been doing homework.

Our standard wager was a nickel a peg. Meaning, if one of us won by 20 pegs, the other person would owe a dollar.

It doesn't sound like big money, and it probably shouldn't have been, but I swear I paid for my first semester of school off cribbage wins.

Cribbage brought us together.

It made us talk. It made us laugh. It made us have some fun.

Cribbage made what could have been a scary part of lives, something that we could handle. Because we played with someone who felt the same way.

A dumb little game did that.

Yeah. Make your own segue.

So, what ever happened to that random freshman roommate?

I see him all the time.

We hang out. We travel together. We play golf. Our kids play and laugh together too.

I've decided that when my son is old enough, I'm teaching him how to play cribbage. Like father like son.

I hope that he plays against my random freshman roommate's son. Because cribbage gave me a friend.

And maybe he'll find one too.

Plus, there's a chance I won't have to pay for his first semester of college.

One of the best parts of golf is what we talked about in the Lego Mentality. There are a lot of pieces that go into golf, but there's not one set way of playing.

Playing 9 or 18 holes is not the only way to play.

You get to create the game. You get to figure out the best way to spend your time with your Dream Group.

Every great game starts with two things: Challenge and Creativity.

During my programs, I give my students a task. It's simple really.

Create a game that we can play as a group.

Everyone gets together with a group to brainstorm and within 5-10 minutes creates a game.

And if you think back to when you were a kid playing with your friends, this is what you did. You created your own challenges with what you had around you. And you came up with your own set of rules, your own boundaries, and your own teams.

There are hundreds of golf games that can be played on the course, on the driving range, on the putting green, in your yard, at the park, and just about anywhere else you can play golf.

Don't limit yourself to the traditional way of playing.

Make the choice to play a different game.

Rick Reilly, who writes for ESPN, put it perfectly, "The best sports are the ones you invent."

Your second pillar of happiness is creating a game that you enjoy the most.

Chapter 17

Happiness Pillar #3: The Location

When Life Gives You Snow

I've told you why I teach golf. (Remember The Night and The Letter?)

Here's why I play golf: to be creative.

When I'm running my business, the answer is the same. I like the freedom to do things that are creative, a little (or a lot) bit different, or out of the ordinary.

And here's the thing...99% of the things I try are complete failures. They don't work. Nobody likes it.

But watch out, cause 1% of the time, I'm deadly...

Due to the constant barrage of snow a few years ago, we had one of the latest springs in Minnesota in a long time. The girls team I coach was getting stir crazy. We couldn't get outside to golf and there was only so much inside practice that we could do. Plus, 3 weeks worth of matches were already cancelled.

But we needed to start playing our matches. Otherwise, we'd never get them in.

By dumb luck, with a foot of snow on the ground, we found a course that was open...even though it was 31 degrees and snowing sideways.

So, I contacted another team to see if they wanted to make up our already cancelled date.

They agreed, and we played.

It was a small course, but had a ton of obstacles. And even though it was fairly dark, many players shot well.

The girls were pumped that they could finally play. For many of them it was the first time ever on a real course.

It was fun watching how precise they were with their shots. In the end, the other team took care of us pretty convincingly.

What course was open in snow and freezing temps?

The laser tag course at Brunswick Zone.

So, yeah, we played laser tag instead of golf that day.

Sometimes, you just have to be creative.

Your third pillar is your location: Where do you want to play?

For most people the much-too-long, way-too-watery championship course is not exactly an ego boost. Yet, people flock to these courses, and then play from a tee box that they have no business playing from.

So, make a different choice.

I have students in my classes that have never been on a real course. Yet, year after year, they play golf with me because they love the driving range and love the chip and putt course.

The location you choose should make you comfortable.

Big course, small course, putting green, driving range, or your own back yard. Pick a spot and play a game.

The beauty of these happiness pillars is that they are interconnected.

The location you choose may determine who you invite and what game you play. Or vice versa. The Dream Group you choose for that day may make a difference in where you decide to play.

Next time your friend says to you, "Hey, let's go golfing," it doesn't mean you have to go to a course. Grab a drink and putt for a while. Go relax at the driving range. Bank golf balls off trees at the park.

Choose a spot that you can enjoy the game.

Chapter 18

Happiness Pillar #4: The Scorecard

I've got some numbers for you.

200.
2.
67.
0.
10,000.
1.

These are some of my golf scores.

There is not just one way to keep score. There is not just a scorecard and a number on each hole.

If you let your scorecard drive your happiness, then you are headed for disaster. Instead, measure your golf game in different ways.

My numbers?

200 Number of golf balls I found during a round with my dad.
2 Number of kids I have that love to golf with me.
67 My career low round.
0 Number of my students that have made it to the PGA Tour.
10,000 Number of students that I've taught over the last 15 years.
1 Number of beverage cart girls that I married.

You've got a few options when it comes to keeping score.

1. Don't keep score.
2. Keep score a different way.
3. Add up every shot you take, let the scorecard control you, and eventually hate golf.

The Nerds

Fenwick Mugglesweater.

That was the answer I got.

The question was, "What should I name the Scottish-looking dude in my logo?"

Most kids said, "Jimmy" "Dylan" "Jack"

But one kid said, "Fenwick Mugglesweater."

Ah, the nerds.

I use that term in a genuinely heartfelt way because I am a nerd and I'm proud of it.

There was this group of kids who were all friends from school/growing up.

None of them were exceptional athletes, but they didn't care.

Either did we.

None of them had any plans of doing much with golf, but they didn't care.

Either did we.

All of them were scared of girls.

So were we.

These guys were awesome. And even though I haven't seen any of them for a few years, I know they're still awesome.

They were one of our first teams in our Team Golf program and they epitomized (biggest word I'll ever use) what a team should be...and what golf should be about.

They laughed with each other. They strategized with each other. They made fun of each other. They congratulated each other.

And they were smart.

Man, were they smart.

Any one of them could program anything on a computer...easily...and well. They would make fun of each other for not knowing C++. (I'm still not sure what that is)

And the nerds asked the greatest question I have ever heard in one of my camps.

"Can we do the Iwo Jima with the golf flag?"

I knew exactly what they were talking about. (Google Iwo Jima Flag if you don't know).

"Of course you can do the Iwo Jima...because it's awesome that you know what that is."

So they took the flag from the 9th hole and "did the Iwo Jima."

The nerds were creative and funny. They had no problem talking Star Wars, school work, or Java Script.

They cared about the games and the competition, but not the winning. They wanted to try their best, but when they went home, they'd do something else and forget about golf.

And they never used a scorecard to keep score.

They knew they would have fun no matter how they played. And they didn't need a number on a card to tell them that.

Keep score in a different way.

Put smiley faces and frowny faces on the card. Count how many golf balls you find. Play match play. Play "first one in the hole." Do something different.

Go be a nerd.

Chapter 19

Hey Zebra

In 9th grade, I realized that I wasn't going to make it to the NBA. Not because of lack of heart or effort. No.

It was mostly because there weren't many white kids, who couldn't jump over a crayon box, or make a left handed layup, that were in the NBA.

So I did what my dad did.

I became a basketball referee.

I learned a few things early on that really stood out.

I learned time management. I learned responsibility. I learned public speaking (cause everyone is always looking at you). I learned how to diffuse tense situations.

I consulted my brain trust and my two main reffing partners (my dad and bro) and we got to talking about all the things we learned through the years.

I came up with The 13 Things That I Learned Reffing Basketball:

1. When a coach is constantly yelling "Thieves in the night!!" "Thieves in the night!!" "Thieves in the night!!" he just wants his players to try and steal the ball.

2. If your brother throws out a coach and a fan for arguing and running on the floor, your tires will get slashed.

3. The best way to address a coach who is getting out of hand is, "Are you this rude at home too?" because it cannot be answered without making the coach look like a total tool.

4. Baseball, Football, and Hockey games are not the only sports that end in a shutout.

5. Orange is not spelled O-R-N-A-G-E (which is how a dad spelled it on the sign he was holding when he was cheering for the "orange" team during the championship game).

6. It is 100% certain that no parent knows or understands the over and back rule.

7. When you are driving home and it seems particularly cold that day, it's because the hole in your pants, that you never noticed during your 4 games, is 6 inches long.

8. Most games are ended when the clock goes off, but some are decided when 3 moms run on to the court to break up fights...during a church league.

9. If all 6 of your games are forfeits during the 1998 Vikings playoff game, then you have two options. One: Watch the game on a small TV set up in the teachers' lounge with the school custodian. Two: Practice hitting each other in the head with chairs, a la WWE. We did both.

10. When Jesse Ventura constantly yells at you during his daughter's game, simply explain to him that it's not your fault that his daughter is shooting at the wrong basket.

11. On a scale of 1 to crap: 7th grade girls' basketball.

12. At the end of the Athlete's prayer, St John Bosco prays for us. And St. John Skavnak, St. John Belushi, and St. Jon Bon Jovi also pray for us.

13. The best thing to say when a player throws up on the floor is "Not It."

But over and above any of the goofy things we learned, we also learned one huge thing...

How to handle situations.

Every situation was different. We had happy fans and crazy fans. We had smart coaches and dumb coaches. We had close games and blowouts. Every game had different things that happened.

And after refereeing for all those years, we found that many of the solutions to the situations were the same.

We were transparent and explained our calls.
We admitted when we were wrong.
We were tough when we needed to and gentle when we didn't.
We listened to concerns.
We made hard decisions.
We made the game about the kids, and nothing else.

Refereeing prepared me for a lot of what I've faced in life. Situations may be different, but people and solutions tend to be the same.

And that's the key to consistency.

It's realizing that every situation is different. The grass, the wind, your thoughts, everything, it's all different.

The holy grail of golf seems to be finding consistency. But consistency doesn't just mean that you hit the same shot over and over again.

Even though situations are always different, it's important to be consistent in how you approach each situation. It goes back to controlling probabilities, not outcomes. Be consistent with how you play the game (probability) and there's a stronger likelihood that you will be happier (outcome).

Consistency is not a myth. We just tend to look at the wrong meaning of it.

So, let's begin to build some consistency by addressing situations on the golf course. They are made up of 3 parts:

1. Building your Library of Shots
2. Creating Comfort
3. Reacting and Adapting

Chapter 20

Building Your Library

Imagine you own an old abandoned library.

You drive up to see what it looks like...

The place is rough around the edges. Bricks are falling off. Paint is chipping. The grass is grown up over the windows. And weeds are sticking through the cracks. Benches are broken and flowers are dead.

So you walk inside and check it out.

Inside looks great.

The floors are polished. The lights are bright. The shelves are cleaned. You never would have guessed from looking at the outside, but this place is awesome.

Except there's one major problem.

There are no books.

It's clean and bright, but empty.

A library without books is not going to work too well.

The place looks like a wreck from the outside and the inside has no books.

You own the library...so what do you do?

How are you going to get people walking down the sidewalk to stop in and check out the library?

You could start by replacing the bricks, painting the outside, mowing the grass, trimming the weeds, fixing the benches, and planting new flowers.

Or....

You could get one book.

See, even though the outside of the building looks immaculate and brand new. And even though what people see may look great, a library still needs books.

A library without books is as good as a restaurant without food.

One book is all you need to start a library.

Your golf swing is like the outside of the library. It can look pretty, but it still might not be of use.

Until you learn how to hit a shot, until you get that one book, the library doesn't work.

And one book can turn into two books. Then 4 books, then 10 books.

Pretty soon, your library is getting filled with books. And when you need something, you can rely on those books for the knowledge to help you out.

Throughout the years, the outside of the library may be beaten by storms, or graffiti, or things beyond your control.

But if the inside is taken care of, and the books are handled well, you'll always have a library.

Here are 4 shots for your library.

The 4 Common Shots

Remember these numbers.

25 million.

250.

There are around 25 million golfers in the U.S. right now.

There are around 250 players on the PGA Tour.

250 guys that play golf for their job.

250 awesome, flawless swings.

24,999,750 swings that aren't good enough for the PGA Tour.

Yet, the majority of teaching is still centered around the swing. Teachers trying to get you do a certain move, or put you side-by-side with Tiger to expose what you'll never be able to do anyway.

Isn't there a better way?

In life, we try to prepare our children for what they may face. We give them our experience. We tell stories about what happened to us and other people we know. We give them insight. We share perspective.

We need to teach situations, not swings.

Golf, like life, is situational.

And it should be taught that way.

Every time you are on the golf course, you are confronted with a situation. Sometimes you're hitting a tee shot. Sometimes you're in a bunker. Sometimes you're in the woods. Sometimes you have great playing partners. Sometimes they are miserable.

For golf, the situation just calls for a different type of shot. Or a different type of thought.

Really, that's what golf is about....Shots and Thoughts.

If you can do these things at a high level, you are going to love golf. You are going to be happy. You are going to be consistent.

If you focus too much on swing, you're going to struggle.

I could share with you hundreds of different situations that happen on the golf course. There are countless numbers of shots that can be taken.

But from my years of study and research, there are really only 4 shots you need right now.

Here are the first 4 shots in your library:

1. **The Putt** - Start Here. Learn to roll it.
2. **The Tee Shot** - Your first shot of each hole, typically from a tee.
3. **The Full Swing Shot** - This is your comfortable full swing shot with whatever club you choose.
4. **The Short Shot** - This is a shot that's less than a full swing.

Are there variations of each of these shots, or each of these situations? Absolutely. But you encounter those less often. If you are looking to improve golf skill, then these are the 4 to remember.

And keep it simple.

During my programs, you'll rarely hear long explanations about the mechanical side of the swing. It's a brain-clogger. You'll hear me say three important things about what we're doing.

I like threes.

I can remember stuff like that.

There are three Stooges.

There are three moves in Paper Rock Scissors (although some would argue Lizard, Spock).

There are three members in Ben Folds Five.....go figure.

I use the word Trifecta when describing the three.

Here is the basic Skill Trifecta for the backswing and the followthrough. I start the skill portion of golf with this to build a base. From there we explore the 4 situations.

Backswing Trifecta:

Relax Your Hands
If you death grip your club, your hands are going to cry and your shots won't be good. You're not here to work. Let the club do that.

Make an L
When you bring the club back, your left arm (for righties) and the club will make the letter L. That's all you need. You're loading up your power. Imagine trying to throw a ball without bending your elbow. Or kicking a ball without bending your knee. That's why we make an L.

Swing
Just swing the club. Let it happen. Don't try to perfect anything. Don't try to guide anything. Just let it go.

Followthrough Trifecta:

Toe
When you are done swinging (or letting it go...way too much Frozen soundtrack), get up on your back toe (right toe for righties).

<u>Shoulder</u>
After your toe is up, make sure your club (hands, grip..same thing) is by your shoulder (left shoulder for righties). This is huge in "letting it go." If you can't get it to your shoulder, there is tension somewhere.

<u>Freeze</u>
When you're done swinging, just stop. Freeze. Watch the ball and where it lands. This teaches balance.

Toe, Shoulder, Freeze is what I've been teaching for 15 years. It's very basic. It's easy to remember. It makes it look like you belong on TV. And it works.

The Trifecta is huge. Keep it simple.

Now let's jump into the 4 shots for your library.

The Putt

Back in the mid-90's, my family took a trip to Florida. We were going to do the whole Disney thing, play a round of golf or two, and hang out.

Our flight was scheduled to leave at 6am. Although, our Minnesota weather decided to dump an ice storm on us the night before, and it continued into the next day.

Our flight was delayed. First, for a couple hours. Then, for a couple more. Eventually, we were set to leave at 3pm...a 9 hour delay.

I had a lot of time to kill.

In the mid-90's I always had one thing with me. My brother would say an awkward fashion sense or weird face. But, no, think dorkier. I always carried a deck of cards with me.

That deck of cards is the reason I have confidence to make any putt I look at now.

Here's why...

During the delay, I took my Chicago Bulls hat off and placed it on the ground about 5 feet away. I grabbed the deck of cards and started tossing cards into the hat. At first, only a couple would go in. Then, after some more time, I could get up to 10. (Remember a deck of cards has 52 cards, plus a couple jokers).

After only a few hours, I was consistently throwing 40-45 cards in the hat.

I could see the path the card needed to take to fall into the hat.

I had found visualization. I had found rhythm. I had started to build some confidence.

I kept moving the hat further away, or behind a garbage can, or under a chair. Sure it was more difficult to make them in, but I got some. I kept seeing how the card needed to move to get to the hat.

I probably threw cards into that hat for 6 hours.

It was the key to developing my "touch" (and probably more dorkiness).

So, years later, when I was developing some putting games for my classes, I remembered back when I threw those cards. Making a card into the hat had nothing to do with me thinking about mechanics. It was just letting my body figure out what it needed to do.

The first thing I do with all my classes is ask each student to roll a ball to the target. Try to get the ball somewhere near the target. After a few throws, you'll have the feeling of how much energy it takes.

Then we move on to using the putter.

Early on, I learned a perfect way to develop "touch" for my students from a colleague of mine named Dan DeMuth.

We putted 4 different ways.

1. One-handed (dominant hand)
2. Two-handed
3. Two-handed with eyes closed
4. Two handed looking at the target

Each of these ways helps you understand how much it takes to get the ball rolling from one place to another.

And "playing catch" is the best way. Do it with a partner. Putt back and forth to each other. Don't use a hole. Take out the golf stuff, so your mind isn't concentrating on making it in the hole. Just get the rhythm down. Feel what it's like first. Check out the slopes and how the ball rolls. Pay attention and observe.

Putting is personal. Like many things in golf, there is no right way to do it. Lego Mentality. Your body will figure out how to move the ball from one place to another.

The Tee Shot

In reality, you don't use the driver much compared to other clubs. When you play 9 holes, you'll use it 6-8 times. Maybe.

But there's something about hitting a long drive, or outdriving your buddies, or doing something you didn't think you could do, that makes it fun and starts to build confidence.

1. Tee the ball high (higher than the top of the club).
2. Place the ball off the front foot.
3. Stand further back than you think (extension is huge for the tee shot).

The Full Swing Shot

You hit your tee shot somewhere forward. Nice work. Now, most likely, you'll have a full swing with some other club.

Let's keep it simple again.

1. Relax your hands
2. Hit down (This is a huge point. You are not trying to lift the ball up. You are hitting down on the ball and letting the club lift it).
3. Followthrough

The Short Shot

This shot is used when you're closer to the green. It has two variations. A high shot and low shot.

Here's the high one...

1. Relax your hands
2. Make an L
3. Hit down

Here's the low one...

1. Feet close
2. Ball back in your stance
3. Choke down on the club

Now, I get it. This is the super-fast, super-simple explanation of each of these shots. We explore these in each of my programs including The Happiest Golfer.

4 Shots is all you need to open your library.

This is the foundation of the skill portion of golf. As you have seen before this chapter, we focus much more on setting yourself up for fun before the skills are even introduced. Like it first, learn it later.

But it's a good start to put some shots in your library.

Chapter 21

Creating Comfort

When I first started teaching, I was 19. I was a sophomore in college and I didn't know much.

Sure, I was playing on my college team. I could shoot in the 70's. But I had never TAUGHT golf before. I had just played it.

My very first lesson I ever taught was an 8-10 year old Park and Rec class. I was terrified.

I was supposed to teach for 45 minutes. A few days before my class, I wrote out on a blank piece of paper what I was going to teach during the class.

I had grip, stance, alignment, posture, half swing, and full swing using irons and woods. I had everything planned out minute by minute. It was exactly 45 minutes. I practiced in front of the mirror the night before class. Perfect. I was ready.

On the day of the class, I introduced myself to my students. They told me their names too. And we started.

You know how when you are nervous, you tend to talk faster than usual?

On that first day of class, my mouth was moving like it had never talked before. My perfectly planned out 45 minutes took about 20.

Uh oh.

What the heck was I going to do for the last 25 minutes?

I had no idea.

The students kept hitting golf balls, and I walked up to them and helped them hit it a little straighter or a little further.

They kept hitting, I kept encouraging.

"Great shot Tyler"
"Sweep that ground Abby"
"Whoa, look how far that went Andrew"

The kids would smile. I would smile.

And then it was over.

The kids went home and so did I.

The first lesson of my career didn't go as I planned. And I wasn't prepared enough to adapt when I had time left in the lesson.

But that was the beauty of it.

Because that first lesson taught me a lot.

It made me reflect on everything that happened during that 45 minutes.

I made mistakes. I didn't plan well enough. I could be much better.

But one huge thing came out of that first lesson that didn't even cross my mind before that night.

And it wasn't until a few years later that I realized this huge secret would be the key to the rest of my career.

Moms Know Everything

My dad is on my weekly email list. Rarely does he comment back with anything (you wouldn't either if you only typed with one finger). But, on one occasion, he wrote this:

Bryan,

Other kids liked school because of mom. She had a way of making them feel comfortable. Especially the little ones.

She would learn the names of all the First Graders, the New Kids On The Block, including their middle names. At lunch time [yes, she was a longtime Lunch Mom too!] she would greet them. "Hi Bryan Michael or Hello Ella Mae" was a greeting heard by each one as they came through the lunch line. Later on, as she learned birthdays, the greeting would expand to "Hi Ethan John, Happy Birthday to you!"

She didn't share her secret with them. The little ones and some older ones too asked, "How did you know it's my Birthday?" She would just smile and often gave them a big Mom hug and say, "Moms know everything." You heard that same phrase often enough. Before you returned home from school, she knew every thing that went on that day because she chatted with everyone, including the school custodians.

Learning middle names, birthdays, names of brothers and sisters were all part of her diabolical scheme to make each person she met, whether big or little, feel at ease and comfortable. She cared. It was one of her biggest gifts which drew so many, many people close to her.

By the way, her secret of learning names and birthdays: Study, study, study. While acting as Nurse Mom in that office, she would study the Medical information cards where names, birthdays, ailments and other private stuff was kept. Maybe she stretched the Right to Privacy rules a little, but as a somewhat scared little child, surrounded by big people in a new environment, she brought comfort and joy!

It took me years to figure this out. But as a teacher, I realized that I wasn't supposed to tell everyone what to do all the time. My job was not to be a fixer and correct every mistake.

My job was to create comfort.

The last 25 minutes of that first class was spent encouraging the kids by name (that's huge) and relating (by laughing a lot) with them.

Comfort is something that everyone cherishes. It's simple. When we're comfortable, we're able to enjoy the situation more and perform better. We're able to understand what's happening. We're able to focus on the things that matter. And most of all, we're able to eliminate fear that holds us back.

Comfort comes in many forms. Everyone has a different idea of what makes them comfortable.

In my 15 years of teaching, I've found you'll respond best to one main comfort.

Relate golf to something you already know.

This is why I always ask the question, "What else do you like to do besides golf?"

My students chatter away about their hobbies and my brain starts working. And I create Relatable Skills.

Relatable Skills

I had a lesson with a guy about 10 years ago and I asked what I thought was an innocent question, "What do you think about when you swing?"

His response was this, "A lot. Here are the 12 things."

And then he recited all 12 things.

Wow.

Do you think the best players in the world and the happiest players in the world think about 12 things when they swing? From years of study, I've found that the best and happiest think of nothing when they swing.

Nothing.

No swing thoughts.

You might think this seems impossible. But it's not. Because they do something else instead.

They relate golf to something else. And they practice and play that way.

Oh, Nuts

Before I played golf, I was a baseball kid.

I loved it.

Lots of teams. Lots of games. And best of all, lots of games of catch with my dad.

Our after dinner routine was usually to go outside and play catch until dark. It was awesome. We would throw fastballs, and attempt to throw curves. Sometimes we'd mix in a change up. But the pitch I loved the most was the knuckleball.

Quick overview of the knuckleball. It comes out of your hand with no spin, so the ball looks like its wobbling at you. It's a tough pitch for batters to hit and for catchers to catch.

My dad had learned to throw the knuckleball from his Uncle Joe. And he was pretty darn good at it. So, he taught me.

I'll refrain from the mechanics of it, but after a few nights, I got pretty decent at throwing the knuckleball. My dad would have to move every once in a while to figure out where it was going.

One night, after dinner, we were playing our usual round of catch. I started to mix up the pitches a bit. My dad didn't know which one was coming. But he was good at reacting.

Fastball - caught it.
Curveball - caught it.
Change up - caught it.

Then I broke out the knuckleball.

To this day, my dad says it was the best knuckleball I've ever thrown.

The ball came out of my hand with absolutely no spin. It was just floating through the air to my dad. It was almost like slow motion. His glove was trying to react to where the ball would end up.

He didn't react fast enough.

Because that knuckleball hit him directly in the...

Yeah.

I hit my dad in the nuts with a knuckleball.

He let out some words I'd never heard before and doubled over. So, I instantly did what any kid would do in that situation.

I laughed my face off.

And I kept laughing and laughing and laughing.

When I first started golf, I knew much more about baseball. So, I took what I knew from baseball and applied it to my golf game.

Baseballs and golf balls hop similarly through the grass. This helped with my chipping. I played many different positions in the infield with different throwing distances. This helped with my lag putting.

The number of things that you already know how to do is endless when it relates to golf.

I challenge you to take the things you are already good at and see how it can be applied to golf.

For baseball players, I do this:

Imagine a baseball field out in front of you. Let's practice hitting it to different parts of the field. Left field. Right field. Over the shortstop's head. Home run to center field.

For tennis players, I do this:

Imagine a tennis court in front of you. Hit a ball to the Ad court. Hit a ball to the Deuce court. If you want your ball to curve left, just hit a top spin forehand. Need some backspin on the ball, hit a drop shot over the net.

For dancers and gymnasts, I do this:

Imagine you're doing a show. What music is playing? Let's feel the rhythm of that music in our golf swing. Let's hum and sing. The tension starts to leave because you're focusing on the music.

See where I'm going with this?

There are things that you know how to do better than golf.

So, relate what you're good at back to golf. Take what you already know and apply it to something you don't.

Just watch out for knuckleballs.

Chapter 22

Reacting and Adapting

In college, we played a golf game called BMW.

BMW stood for B*tch, Moan, Whine.

The game worked like this...

For every shot that you hit on the golf course, if you B, M, or W'd, and the shot ended up okay (not even good, just at least okay), then you had to hit your shot over again.

For example, after hitting your drive, if you complained that it didn't feel good, or went too far right, or didn't end up like you thought, but still was a decent shot...you had to hit it again.

The game was great because it made you realize what came out of your mouth every time you hit a shot.

Guess what? Every shot will not be perfect. But it may be perfectly acceptable.

Hitting a bad shot is fine. It's your reaction to that shot that matters.

The Burn

I've taught next to a jail for 15 years. The golf facility is actually run by the jail. There are inmates who tend to the grounds and pick golf balls.

And really these guys in this jail are just like you and me.

The major difference is that they reacted differently to a situation and it got them in trouble.

At some point, most of us will have had too much to drink. We get someone to take us home. But for some of these guys...instead of calling someone to pick them up after they drank too much, they decided to drive home. They got caught. They got in trouble. Different reaction to the situation.

At some point, most of us will get in an argument with someone we love. We say bad things. Then we cool off. But for some of these guys...instead of walking away and cooling off, they decide to take a swing at the person they love.

At some point, most of us will really want something that we can't afford. We wait until we have enough money to get it, or we never do get that thing. But for some of these guys...instead of waiting, they decide to steal that thing.

Adjacent to the driving range is the jail. And this jail operates like a workhouse. Inmates are expected to either work on various crews (laundry, janitorial, kitchen, and others) or sit in their cell during the day.

I heard this story from an officer inside the jail...

The guys working on the kitchen crew are known to steal different food items and bring them back to their cells. So, at different times throughout the week, the inmates are searched for contraband.

One night, the kitchen crew was wrapping up and was told to line up to be searched.

Everyone lined up, and the officer began the search.

After searching a few guys, he noticed the last guy in line began to fidget around. He had a cringed face and was moving strangely. Almost like an uncomfortable dance. (Like the 38 year old dude in the club who doesn't really know how to Dougie).

The officer continued the search and finally made it to the fidgety guy. By now the guy was in some sort of pain.

The officer began the search on him and felt something near his inner thigh (it's a family book - don't get alarmed). The officer reached into the front of the inmate's pants and pulled out... a chicken fried steak.

The inmate was doing the dance of pain because that chicken fried steak was piping hot. And it ended up burning a round circle on his inner thigh.

So, what's the moral?

Don't steal.

Don't put hot food down your pants.

More importantly, when confronted with a situation, think about it, and react in a reasonable way.

Casey

Back in high school, I worked at a jail. Yep, the same jail that I teach golf at now.

But, back before there were duck races, chipping contests, and happy golfers, there was me and a couple friends, and a facility that needed a lot of general maintenance.

We painted. We mowed grass. We cleaned. We hauled stuff away. We did just about everything.

It was a great job. And we were put in a lot of different situations.

A few of the things I learned:

1. If you run over a paint can with a Geo Metro on your first day of work, not only will the paint can get stuck to the bottom of the car, but the streak of red paint on the asphalt makes the parking lot look like a crime scene.

2. The larger the man, the faster the sprint, when he accidentally weed whips a bee hive.

3. If you put a stop sign on the wrong side of the post, no one will stop, and everyone will make fun of you.

4. Tuesday's burgers are usually the same as Wednesday's beef stew.

5. I do not have tuberculosis.

We also learned life lessons. Work hard, stay on task, respect authority, and be on time.

Every morning, my friends and I would drive together to work. On one particular morning, my friend Casey overslept. This just happened to be his third day of work. We didn't want to be late, so we left without Casey.

He showed up about 20 minutes late and went straight to my dad's office to apologize.

My dad is a teddy bear. Big dude, generous heart, and a smart guy.

After Casey came back out of my dad's office, we all were curious what my dad said.

Because there was work dad and there was home dad. This doesn't mean good and bad. It was just two different mentalities. And it had to be done that way. Because my dad was the warden of a 400 bed, 125 staff jail. He needed to be a leader. His personality was the same, but his demeanor was different. Do a good job, take some risks, and do good for his employees.

"What did he say?"

"Well, he told me that it wasn't that big of a deal. People oversleep. Everyone is allowed to oversleep. But if it happens again, I'm fired."

Wake up call.

From that moment on, we were always 15 minutes early. We weren't even close to oversleeping again.

Teachable moment.

My dad was calm and cool. He just said what needed to be said. This situation could have been handled in multiple ways, but he chose to make an uncomfortable situation comfortable by reacting and adapting in a way that helped us learn.

We are all confronted with situations. Golf and life are the same. Just a bunch of situations.

What defines us is how we react and adapt to situations.

Chapter 23

My Reminder

There was this old animated show on MTV called 3-South.

It was about a couple of guys (who were idiots) and their experience as freshman at college.

There was one kid in line at the cafeteria who said, "Okay, I'll have one asparagus, and one asparagus, and one asparagus, and one asparagus. How many is that? Eleventy-blue?"

That is going to make more sense than what you read next.

My mom died on May 24, 2011.

About 6 months after my she died, I started going crazy.

Not crazy in a bad way. Just a weird crazy.

See, I started seeing things.

More specifically, I started seeing patterns.

Even more specifically, I started seeing patterns of 11s.

Freaking everywhere.

It started with time.

I would glance up at the clock and see it was 11:11am.

Then later on, I'd glance again, and it was 2:11. Then 3:11. Then 4:11.

There was one day that I saw every 11 between 11:11am and pm.

It was weird to say the least.

I went to Target and bought 4 bags of Jolly Rancher suckers for my classes. The total?

$11.11

I went to Lunds and bought an assortment of stuff. Apples, cucumbers, a watermelon, and couple other things. The total?

$11.11

The very next time I went to Lunds, I went on a big grocery run. The total?

$68.89

Broke the streak, right?

Nope.

See, I always pay for groceries with cash. I gave the lady 4 twenties. My change?

$11.11

I just laughed when she handed me my change.

I didn't know what was going on. And I didn't tell anyone about it. I just kept observing. And I thought about the number 11 more.

I was born on the 11th day. So was my daughter.

My mom was born in the 11th month. So was my son.

And it continued...

The next spring, my kids had an all-class play that they were going to see. My wife couldn't go, so I invited my dad. I had never been to this theater before, so I googled it to find the address.

1111 Mainstreet.

A few weeks later, I needed to make a tee time around 10am for a group. I called and asked for the time.

"Sorry sir, the only time we have left is 11:11."

Of course it is.

This continued for almost a year.

Still I had never told anyone.

My dad came over to my place one Saturday afternoon to play with the kids. He was going to church right from my house, so we were keeping an eye on the time.

We were sitting on the couch and he asked me, "Hey, what time is it?"

I looked over at the oven clock and it read 4:11.

I just shook my head, chuckled, and said, "It's 4:11. Of course it is."

Then he said something I will never forget:

"Have I ever told you about my eleven thing?"

"What?" I said.

He went on to tell me, "Ever since mom died, I've seen elevens everywhere I look."

Mind blown.

For the last year, on clocks, in stores, on odometers, bank statements, casino payouts...everywhere. He had seen elevens.

And neither one of us had said a thing to anyone.

To this day, we still see elevens everywhere we look.

Dad made a deposit on a new house...the check number was 11011.

The new address of that house. 10451. Add up the digits. Yep, 11.

I helped him pay a bill online last month...confirmation number had 10 digits, and smack in the middle was 1111.

After my daughter's kindergarten screening 3 weeks ago, we walked back out to the car and had to stop for a school bus to go by. The bus number was 111.

And the kicker... two weeks ago, on my parents' anniversary, before I went to bed, I re-read the original email I wrote about mom. I had filed it away.

It was 11:41pm.
Story 11 or 11.
And I had 11% left on my phone.

So am I crazy?

I don't think so.

Ever since I started writing, I've been telling you that the most important lesson my mom ever taught me was perspective.

She showed me how to view things.

So, no, I'm not crazy.

It's just a reminder. And we all need reminders at some point.

Remember she died on May 24, 2011.

5/24/11

5+2+4 = 11

11/11

Chapter 24

Your Reminder

It's time for Happy Golf. It's time for a Happier You.

But when learning something new, you may struggle a bit at first. Although most things will be minor inconveniences.

Stick with it. You'll be glad you did.

But just in case, here's your reminder.

You'll face one big obstacle when building your foundation...

The game becomes bigger than the group.

There will be times when you'll lose your perspective and think that the skill of golf is more important than the people you are with. It happens a lot. It has happened to me.

Now granted, you are trying to improve. You are trying to get better. But don't isolate your group for that sake.

Keep your Dream Group in mind.

Club slammers, club throwers, swearers (it's a word now)...they make the game bigger than the group.

I've been each of those people. But I've learned. I've continued to get better.

Especially after the chicken incident of 1990.

Did I Really Just Lose to A Chicken At Tic Tac Toe?

Dumb chicken.

My family has a few traditions.

One awesome tradition is a family vacation every year during the last week in July. We travel to northern Minnesota and have a good old time golfing, swimming, and eating our weight in ice cream. This has been a 30 year tradition. And now my kids get to jump in on the fun.

When I was younger, we'd always stop at a place called Paul Bunyan Land. I live in Minnesota so think of it as a smaller, less exciting, more flannel Disneyland.

When I was 12, we stopped at Paul Bunyan Land, went on a few rides, ate a corn dog or 10, and walked around the place.

Then I saw it.

Although at first, I didn't know what IT was.

I could see a chicken. And I could see a Tic Tac Toe game. And somehow they were connected.

As I got closer, I noticed that the chicken was inside a cage and an electronic Tic Tac Toe game was facing out, so someone could play against the chicken.

It worked like this...

You put in a quarter and somehow chicken feed would be put in 9 slots on a board. These 9 slots are what represented the Tic Tac Toe board. Then, the chicken and the player would take turns playing. When it was the chicken's turn, it would peck the chicken feed from one of the slots on the board. And by doing this, a red X lit up. It was all random and not exactly high tech. But it interested me and I wanted to see how it worked.

I know the whole thing sounds weird. But remember, in the early 90's in Minnesota we had Kirby Puckett. And that's about it. This Tic Tac Toe chicken thing could have been the second best thing going on.

I put in my quarter and the chicken went first. (That is the weirdest sentence I have ever written).

The chicken pecked and a red X lit up. I clicked a button to place the O. We took turns until that fateful move.

Dumb chicken.

I just stood there in shock.

The chicken beat me at Tic Tac Toe.

In my defense, the lights were not working on the game, so I couldn't tell which slots were X's and O's. Or which slots were previously taken.

But that didn't matter to my mom, my dad, and my brother, who absolutely let me have it.

They ripped me so hard. They heckled and taunted, and wouldn't let up.

I was the Yankees at Fenway. I was Nickelback anywhere. But most of all, I was the idiot who just lost to a chicken in Tic Tac Toe.

And I was not happy.

I couldn't tell if I wanted to cry or punch that chicken in the face.

I didn't do either.

I just got heckled. And couldn't do anything about it.

I tried to fight back, defend myself, and make excuses. I got mad at my family.

But the reality was...

It was my own fault. I was responsible for what happened. No outside forces summoned the chicken to kick my butt.

Thank God I'm more grounded than when I was 12. I can laugh about it, and relate it back to my golf game years later.

The loss to the chicken actually helped my golf game. Because I let that one dumb game ruin my day with my family.

Here's the secret...

If you can go into any situation and realize that everything that happens is completely up to you, then you can be happy.

I'm not saying that everything you want to happen is going to turn out exactly how you want it to. I'm saying that if you can accept full responsibility for everything that happens to you, make no excuses, and place no blame, then you are on your way to becoming truly happy.

Because responsibility is just a challenge. It's a challenge to make ourselves a little better.

It's easy to blame other people or make excuses when things don't turn out in our favor.

You know those people who say that there are no dumb questions?

Yeah, their opinion is wrong.

I've heard my share of questions before that are crazy, funny, weird, and kind of dumb.

But nothing compares to one I saw on TV recently.

In the morning, I drop off my kids at preschool and head over to Lifetime to work out.

I start by grabbing one of the ellipticals facing the 27,000 TVs and proceed to run for 45 minutes.

Now, in that 45 minutes, and with those 27,000 TVs, I get to scan a lot of morning shows. I always have music blaring in my ear (sorry mom), so I read the closed captioning.

There's the Price is Right, the Queen Latifah show, SportsCenter, and every political show known to man.

Whichever political show that was on had a question of the day.

Brace yourself...

"Who would you blame if the government had to shut down?"

Now, this is no political thing. I'm not here to debate your political beliefs.

This a dumb question thing.

Seriously. Who would you blame? What the heck good does that do?

I'm supposed to use my energy to think about who is to blame for something?

So, running on that elliptical, I did the only thing I could think of (plus I had about 28 minutes left)...I related it back to golf.

Because we do this all the time in golf.

We blame. We make excuses.

It's too hot. It's too cold. My ball was in a divot. The greens are too fast. The lawnmower dude wouldn't shut off his mower. My club was dirty. The beverage cart girl was too cute. My hair hurts.

You know what?

Buck up.

If it's too cold, put on a jacket.
If the greens are too fast, putt it softer.
If your club is dirty, clean it.
If your ball landed in a divot, it's because you hit it there.
And guess what? If you lose to a chicken at Tic Tac Toe, it's because you didn't play well enough.

Take responsibility. And do it for everything.

You want to get better at golf? Find a coach.
You want to be a great putter? Practice more.
You want to be happier? Start today.

Blame makes no sense.

It doesn't matter what caused it.

Take responsibility for what happens in your golf game. This is part of the foundation that we need.

I never realized the feeling of freedom you get when you can play the game without any blame. It took a long time for me to figure this out.

When my ball would go in a divot, I'd automatically be frustrated and feel like it was bad luck. But in reality, I hit it there. It was my fault. It was much easier to move on and forget about what just happened when I readily admitted that I caused that situation.

Your past shots have no effect on your future shots, so why think about what just happened? New situation. New shot. Move on.

And be proud of the times you made a birdie. Or you made an awesome recovery shot. Or you hit a booming drive. Don't discount your value. You can do great things.

Take responsibility for your actions in life. And also take responsibility when things go well. Sure, you're going to have your share of screw-ups, but you'll have many more times when things go great. And you are the reason they went great. That's part of your responsibility too.

So, how do we overcome a potential loss of perspective? How do we make sure that losing to a chicken at Tic Tac Toe doesn't make you swear off Buffalo Wild Wings? How do we make sure that our relationship and connection with our Dream Group remains more important than a score or a swing?

The Fortunate 5

After years and years of watching my mom play cards, and spend time with her friends, I realized that she was constantly happy in her groups. And happy people tend to have the same qualities.

Happy people remain focused on their Dream Group by doing a few things:

They Give.
They Ask.
They Listen.
They Laugh.
They Play.

In my first book, The Happiest Golfer, I called this The Fortunate 5. These are the 5 things you can do to make sure you remain committed to your Dream Group.

Give - Give of your time. Give help. Give attention. Give a compliment. Give advice. Give a gift. Give affection. Give something that the other person needs to feel happier. Simple as that. Give what you have to other people. This is the first key to any relationship. Even if you don't do anything else on this list, do this one. Give.

Ask - Ask questions. But ask personal questions. Ask about the other person's interests. Ask about feelings, and highs and lows. Ask about dreams and hopes. Ask things that others wouldn't.

Listen - Really listen. Be there to listen whenever it's needed. Listen for details or hints or small things. The more you listen, the more you're able to ask.

Laugh - Find the humor in every situation. Smile and laugh...but really mean it.

Play - Make things social. Go out for breakfast or lunch. Join leagues. Take up new things. Go to events. Play cards. Play games. Have an avenue to constantly get together...card club, church group, school group.

The Fortunate 5 is what Happy Golf is all about.

There will be bumps in the road. You won't play well. You'll get in arguments. You'll lose to chickens.

But remembering these 5 things will help you regain your perspective and put you down the right path again.

Chapter 25

39 Ways You Can Become a Happy Golfer (and Person) Today

Now's your chance. Dive in. Start today. Heck, start right now. Here are 39 ways that you can become a happy golfer...

1. Don't keep score sometimes.
2. Stop comparing yourself to others.
3. Go get ice cream after your round.
4. Smile more on the course.
5. Keep your head up when you are walking.
6. Get to know the people you are playing with.
7. Wave at the beverage cart girl.
8. Find a golf ball in the pond or the woods.
9. Accept that you hit a bad shot.
10. Play faster.
11. Decide what shot to hit and commit to it.
12. Make up your own rules.
13. Play the entire hole with one club.
14. Be aware of everything else on the course.
15. Stop thinking so much.
16. Relax your grip.
17. Remember your great shots.
18. Ask someone close to you to go play.
19. Putt one handed or with your eyes closed.
20. Tee up every shot.
21. Try to skip a shot across the water.
22. Let your kid drive the cart.
23. Stack two golf balls on top of each other and hit the bottom one.
24. Caddy for your kid.
25. Wear weird golf clothes.
26. Play barefoot.
27. Watch Caddyshack.
28. Play in the rain.
29. Start closer to the hole.

30. Throw your ball out of the sand.
31. Move your ball away from a tree.
32. Skip a hole.
33. Play HORSE.
34. Play speed golf.
35. Sing while you play.
36. Play mini golf.
37. Go somewhere new to play.
38. Learn from someone.
39. Hit another shot if you don't like the first one.

But most of all...

Do Something Different.

Chapter 26

The Hey Mom Letter

I hope this book serves as an important piece of your puzzle in both golf and life. And I hope you find something in this book that helps you become unstuck.

I found my piece and became unstuck, so I wrote another letter about it...

Hey Mom-

I think I figured it out.

I know why you left. I know why it was your time.

Your puzzle was done.

See, over the last few years, I've written a lot about you. I've told people stories that made them laugh and cry. I've told them personal things, and I shared things I never thought I would.

Some people used the words legacy and honor, but I just wanted to show them how happy you really were.

Every one of these stories was from a memory that you gave me. And you know me, remembering to do things isn't exactly my strong suit. But remembering <u>people</u> is way easier to do...especially the ones you love the most.

All the things you told me, all the times we spent together, all the times we laughed and argued and ate ice cream...these are pieces of my puzzle. Some may have been pieces of your puzzle too.

You told me when I was younger, "If you want to be truly rich, you already are if you are happy and good."

Piece of the puzzle.

You watched and cheered all my baseball and basketball games. You walked with me during my golf matches.

Piece of the puzzle.

You sang loud in church even though you said you had a bad voice. (It wasn't that bad...it wasn't Nickelback bad).

Piece of the puzzle.

I've realized that as we go through life, we all have these puzzles that we're trying to create. We have different pieces to fill in.

And these pieces aren't about our egos, and victories, and accomplishments.

No. These pieces are the important people in our lives.

You had the most pieces I had ever seen.

People were always astounded how you could have so many friends. Your funeral was the biggest the church had ever seen.

Your puzzle was huge.

But I know that you worked at that puzzle. You put other people in your life before you...and your puzzle grew.

I'm hoping my puzzle gets to be as great as yours.

Even near the end, you continued to gather pieces of the puzzle. You continued to make an impact on people.

Especially me.

Because when you got sick, and while I was watching you go through your stuff, I started having trouble with my puzzle. I was scared to put myself out there, so that my puzzle could grow.

My puzzle was stuck.

I needed a piece that I didn't have. And I didn't know where to look.

But, always the giver that you are, you again showed me the path.

I know now why you continued to smile all the way to the end.

You were giving me another piece of my puzzle.

I needed to embrace what was happening. I needed to approach things how you approach them. I needed to realize that happiness is all around us. I needed to showcase people.

I needed perspective.

This time, the piece you gave me was your last piece.

Because you knew that when your puzzle was finished, mine could continue to grow.

You knew that the piece that completed your puzzle, was the piece that made mine unstuck.

You are the reason I became unstuck.

You are the most important piece of my puzzle.

Your death was your last piece. You had finished your puzzle.

When your friends and family look at it, they see a whole lot of people, a whole lot of cool memories, and a whole lot of happiness.

And they simply smile.

But even though you're gone...you're still a part of my puzzle.

Thanks for reminding me through all the 11:11 stuff.

I wouldn't have been able to grow my puzzle unless you helped me along. And you're still doing just that. You're giving me memories to share that will make the world happier.

So, I'm trying to continue on what you started: Sharing happiness by giving them a little piece of their puzzle.

Thanks for being the most important piece of mine.

Thanks for showing me the path. Thanks for highlighting all the people in your life. Thanks for showing me what's really important.

Thanks for putting together your puzzle so flawlessly, that only happiness could spring from it.

And thanks for sharing that happiness with others.

Especially me.

Love,
Bryan

P.S. Hope you're having fun.

P.P.S. Since you're up there, ask God why he's letting this #hashtag thing last so long.

Chapter 27

It's Our Time

My life changed a few years ago.

I had everything going for me: great family, great friends, fun career.

Then my mom died.

And since that day, I've done a lot of remembering.

Life is not about the stuff. It's not about the accomplishments. It's not about the promotions. It's not about the golf score. It's not about impressing others.

It's about stories. It's about moments. It's about people.

It's about happy people.

It's about figuring out why.

And that's the ultimate foundation.

Because people like my mom, the happy people, are the ones that you want to be around. They are the ones who can teach you without discouraging. They are the ones who pump you up when things aren't going your way. They are the ones who influence you. They are your mentors, your leaders, and your role models.

They are your Daddy Caddies and your Happy Golfers.

My mom prepared me (and my family) so well throughout her life, that her dying didn't need to be a miserable moment. She was special. She was happy. And she spread that happiness to others.

A few years later, I still have a great family. I still have great friends. I still have a fun career.

But my life changed...because I made a choice to do something different. I wanted to help more. I wanted to do something that encouraged you, made you happier, and challenged you.

So, I wrote "The Letter."

And in those 871 words, my life became a mission. A mission that's bigger than golf. A mission that's bigger than just me.

I didn't know it at the time. But now it's clear.

My mission is to spread happiness.

Life has ways of making you buck up. Life has ways of making you take charge of your actions and saying enough is enough.

Enough of the lack of self confidence. Enough of the fear.

Enough of thinking, but not doing.

Enough of kids being mean to each other. Enough of the fights and arguments. Enough of people being unhappy.

If you're like me, you're sick and tired of the negativity, you're sick of the complaining, you're sick of the blame.

Enough of being scared to share the real you.

Your vulnerability is what connects you to other people.

We don't have to go through life being unhappy.

There is a better way to live. There is real happiness all around us. We just can't be scared to go get it.

This isn't a just golf thing. This isn't just a kids thing. This isn't just a family thing.

This is an us thing.

It's our time to be happy.

We're in this thing together. And we have a job to do.

I use golf as my stage to spread this message. The message of happiness. The message of stronger relationships, deeper connections, and lasting memories.

It starts with us. We need to be stronger for our kids. We need to be more courageous for our families. We need to stick up for our co-workers. We need to smile more, laugh more, love more, care more, and help more.

We need to crush the fear, answer the big questions, and embrace perspective.

You have the set of instructions. But remember, there are rules. And there are no rules. Take the pieces you need to build something great.

It's our time.

Join me and the other happy people. Let's show them that we can be happy.

Let's spread happiness to other people.

Let's be helpful.

Let's make use of our talents.

Let's create what makes us smile.

Let's be the happy ones.

It's our time.

My mom was the epitome of happiness. Before she died, she looked at me and said, "We had a good run, didn't we?"

We're still running, mom.

We're just getting started.

You made it to the last page. Nice work. Thanks for taking the time to read. I appreciate it.

Were there any stories that hit home? Let me know.

If you like the stories in this book, then I've got more for you over at:

www.thehappiestgolfer.com

And I release many more on my Facebook page as well.

Facebook: Bryan Skavnak Golf Academy

Wishing you more happiness on and off the course.

Talk soon,
Bryan

P.S. Keep reading. There's one more bonus story at the end.

The generosity of those below helped make this book a reality.

Alex Wilson
Amy Cerepak
Ann Feitl
Anna Sabiston
Arctic Capital
Avery & Willa Iannazzo
Buck Huot
Calvin Bazal
Charlotte
Chris Donlin
Chris Porisch
Chrisy
Colin Tietz
Cory and Becky McNattin
Dave
Diane Anthony
Dianne Johnson
Erin Addington
Friend of Sandy
Gary
Grace Humphrey
Heather Ward & Family
Heyer Family
Homar
Jackie Santopietro
Janine Skavnak
Joe O'Brien
Joleen Katula
Jonathan & Amy Robinson
Joseph and Krista Masek
Josh Wurzberger
Karl Jaschke
Kathy Karel
Katie Mickelson
Katie Nelson
Keith Sexton
Kelsey Walt
Kevin Younghans

Kyle Woods
Lauren
Lindsey Pederson
Margaret McKibbin
Mark H Johnson
Mark Paluta
Mary & Terry Hunter
Mary Ann Williams
Matt Petschl
Matt Vikander
Michael Sexton
Mike Gengler
Nathan and Heather Maehren
Pat Karel
Pat O'Brien
Paul Kroening
Rick and Kimberly Carlsen
Robert James Ritchie
Rodney Landin
Roger Schwartz
Ron Karel
Sam and Joe Sigel
Schmidty
Scott Noerenberg
Steve & Jen Skavnak
Susan Williams
The Filiaggis
The Greatest College Roommate
The Felien Family - Mike,
Lindsay & Beckham
The Hagan Family
The Reid Family
Theresa Sarafolean
Todd Hildebrandt
Tom Shannon
Tracy Sudak

Be the Ball

Golf is an opportunity.

At least that's what Bill Murray said.

And it means something different to every person.

Throughout the last few years, acclaimed filmmaker Erik Anders Lang has gone inside the ropes to conduct countless interviews to crawl into the minds of those who have a deeper connection to the game; Tour players, world leaders, writers, and more.

What he's finding is extraordinary. And what's even cooler is that he's creating a feature length documentary, called Be the Ball, to expose it all.

What does Rory think? What does Rickie think? What does Jason think?

It's being called the greatest sports experiment ever conducted.

Imagine a story that has made you laugh, cry, and think. A story that has had a profound effect on you. Then multiply it by 100. And add Bill Murray.

Be the Ball is that story.

See more at www.betheballmovie.com

Bonus Story

I am not a fan of snow.

It makes driving difficult, messes up the sidewalks, and makes my socks all wet.

Sure, it looks pretty when it shines in the sun, but so does Kristen Bell, and I don't see her chilling in my front yard all winter.

But snow does make me remember.

Especially to the winter of 2005.

I got an email. An email from Rolling Stone magazine.

I had subscribed to this magazine since I was in high school, so for more than 10 years at $25 a year, I had been up to date on all things music.

This email was an offer for a lifetime subscription.

Cool.

After I clicked on the link, I realized that this lifetime subscription was only $100.

$100 for the rest of my life. No strings attached. (I combed it through...there really were no strings).

So, I took my St. John's math and my calculator and quickly discovered that normally I would spend $100 in 4 years. I consulted my accountant, ran an actuarial analysis, and signed up.

The next month when the Rolling Stone magazine came in the mail, I happened to glance at the address label.

Side note: Did you know that on magazine subscription address labels, there's a line with the expiration date of your subscription?

When I was checking the label, I noticed that my expiration date said, "Sep55."

Huh?

I had just signed up for a lifetime subscription. Why would there be an expiration date?

I'm a reasonable dude, so a few thoughts came to my head...

1. Maybe they just added 50 years to my subscription to make it easy on their computer system? Nope. It was 49 years and 8 months.

2. Maybe that's the date where all paper magazines are required to go digital? Thanks Obama.

3. Maybe Rolling Stone knows when I'm going to die?

Ooohhh (insert creepy music).

But then I came to my senses and realized that's dumb. Nobody knows when their time is up.

Heck, I could walk outside tomorrow and get hit by a Nickelback tour bus. (The coroner would not want to look at that photograph).

So, I really started thinking...

Who is driving that tour bus, me or fear?

Am I going to let fear knock me down?

Or am I going to take control, (drop Nickelback off at the closest rest stop), and create my own tour?

I might have until September 2055.

But what if I don't?

Sometimes we end up waiting our whole lives for something to be perfect before we take that big step. The perfect opportunity, the perfect business plan, the perfect opening line.

If we wait until perfect, then we just push our happiness further down the road.

We can't control the outcome, but we can control the probability.

So, we better do something now.

We better make our opportunity now.

We better care more now.

We better love more now.

We better appreciate more now.

And we better give and live more. Now.

You want a better job? You want a better golf game? You want a better relationship? You want a better life?

Refuse to wait. Refuse to listen to critics. Refuse to let fear stop you.

It's time you understand that you are worth it. You are significant. You matter.

There are no little people.

Do something now. And think big.

We all have something we want.

Go get it.

Happy ~~Golf~~ Life Starts Here.